EXTENDING SCIENCE 11

BIOTECHNOLOGY

Selected Topics

J Teasdale BSc

Stanley Thornes (Publishers) Ltd

Extending Science Series

1 Air   E N Ramsden and R E Lee
2 Water   E N Ramsden and R E Lee
3 Diseases and Disorders   P T Bunyan
4 Sounds   J J Wellington
5 Metals and Alloys   E N Ramsden
6 Land and Soil   R E Lee
7 Energy   J J Wellington
8 Life Worldwide   T Carrick
9 Nuclear Power   R E Lee
10 Forensic Science   T H James
11 Biotechnology   J Teasdale
12 Pregnancy and Birth   S D Tunnicliffe
13 Sport   R B Arnold

Further titles are being planned and the publishers would be grateful for suggestions from teachers.

CONTENTS

Preface v
Acknowledgements vi
Safety vii

Chapter 1 Biotechnology: An Introduction

What is biotechnology? 1
Case study 1 Plant tissue culture and oil-palms 6
Case study 2 Are extinct animals really extinct? 8
Biotechnology: past and future 10
Case study 3 Genetic engineering and human insulin production 16
Summary 21
Activity 1 Tissue culture of potato plants 22
Activity 2 What do you know? 23
Questions on Chapter 1 23

Chapter 2 Living Things and Industrial Processes

Cells and basic biology 25
How enzymes work 27
Case study 4 Enzymes, immobilisation and high fructose syrup 29
Cells and food 31
Cells and oxygen 32
Cells and industrial processes 33
Summary 37
Activity 3 Experiments with washing powders 38
Questions on Chapter 2 39
Crossword on living things and industrial processes 40

Chapter 3 Biotechnology and Food

Microbes and food processing 42
Traditional industries 42
Case study 5 What's English, soft, blue and new? 48
Case study 6 Algae as food 49
Case study 7 Fungi as food 50
Case study 8 Bacteria as food 50
Farms or fermenters? 52
Summary 52
Activity 4 Measuring the densities of liquids – milk and beer 52
Activity 5 Experiments with yoghurt 54
Activity 6 The action of rennin on milk 55
Activity 7 Fungus in cheese 58
Activity 8 Detection of protein in microbial foods 60
Activity 9 A mini Pruteen fermenter 61
Questions on Chapter 3 62

Chapter 4 Biotechnology and Fuels

Plants and energy	65	Case study 12 Put an oil-palm		
Biomass	65	in your tank!		77
Ethanol from biomass	67	Case study 13 More oil from		
Case study 9 Sugar to fuel	68	oil wells		78
Methane from biomass	71	Case study 14 Beyond biomass		80
Case study 10 DIY fuel on		Summary		81
the farm	73	Activity 10 Gas from waste		81
Simple biogas digesters	73	Activity 11 Home-made fuel?		82
Case study 11 Biogas from		Questions on Chapter 4		83
landfill sites	75	Wordfinder on biotechnology		
Biomass, biotechnology, what else?	77	and fuels		84

Chapter 5 Biotechnology and Water

Drinking water	85	Activity 13 What we know	
Waste water	85	about water	92
Case study 15 The deep		Activity 14 Visit a water	
shaft process	90	treatment centre	92
Clean water: some problems	90	Questions on Chapter 5	93
Summary	91		
Activity 12 How much			
water do you use?	92		

Chapter 6 Biotechnology, Health and Disease

Antibiotics	95	Activity 16 Helping Y-US	109
Case study 16 Antibiotic		Activity 17 Using a key to	
production	99	distinguish between products	
Vaccines	104	of biotechnology	110
Case study 17 Magic bullets	106	Questions on Chapter 6	111
Summary	108	Wordmaze on biotechnology,	
Activity 15 Penicillin production	109	health and disease	113

Further Reading

Textbooks	114	Booklets produced by	
		industrial organisations	114

Answers	**117**	**Index**	**118**

PREFACE

Biotechnology is the harnessing of life in order to produce food, drugs or chemicals, or to provide services such as waste disposal. In recent years, biotechnology has become increasingly important. It has the potential to solve major world problems such as famine, disease, fuel supply and pollution. Its impact is such that many people think that biotechnology will be as important tomorrow as computers are today.

Biotechnology holds a central role in science today, and computing, technology, engineering, economics, social issues and politics are all relevant to the subject.

As a topic biotechnology can be included in a number of GCSE and Scottish Standard Grade subjects ranging from Biology, Chemistry, General Science and Technology to Home Economics and Geography. It is also becoming increasingly important in TVEI. This book will be useful for all such courses and will be of interest to those following social sciences, environmental science and general studies courses.

Throughout, I have attempted to deal with a difficult area in a simple way. It is my hope that everyone who uses the book will find it clearly presented and stimulating.

J Teasdale
Birkenhead Sixth Form College,
Wirral

ACKNOWLEDGEMENTS

I would like to thank my wife Susan and children Ruth and Paul, for their encouragement during the writing of this book.

The author and publishers are grateful to the following who provided photographs and gave permission for reproduction:

Barnaby's Picture Library (p. 67);
Beechams (pp. 1(b) and 5);
Biofotos (p. 78);
Brazilian Institute of Sugar and Alcohol (pp. 68, 69 and 70 (top));
Camera Press (p. 91 (top) and 96);
Camera Talks (p. 72 (top));
Eli Lilly Limited (pp. 17, 100, 101 and 102);
Gist Brocades, Holland (p. 13);
ICI Agricultural Division (pp. 1(a), 20, 35(b) and 51);
Merseyside Waste Disposal Authority (p. 75);
N. Francis (p. 76);
National Dairy Council (p. 44);
Natural Science Photos (p. 91 (bottom));
Peter Fraenkel (p. 74);
Philip Harris Biological Ltd (p. 8);
Science Photo Library (p. 49);
Science Photo Library – Alexander Tsiaras (main cover)
– Dr Jeremy Burgess (behind title on cover)
– Hank Morgan (p. 105);
Scientific American, USA (p. 46);
South American Pictures (p. 70 (bottom));
The Mansell Collection (pp. 12, 94, 95 and 104);
WS Tech. Centre (p. 33).
The cartoon on p. 19 first appeared in *New Scientist*, London, the weekly review of science and technology.

Every attempt has been made to contact copyright holders, but we apologise if any have been overlooked.

The main cover photograph shows a biotechnologist making adjustments to analytical equipment connected to a biological fermenter (right). The instrument provides a controlled, sterile environment where genetically engineered micro-organisms can flourish.

The photograph behind the title lettering shows *Penicillin chrysogenum*, 3 days old, grown on potato dextrose agar medium. *P. chrysogenum* was used in early antibiotic production.

ADVICE TO TEACHERS AND TECHNICIANS

Before carrying out any practical work using microbes please consult some or all of the following:

Microbiology – An HMI guide for schools and non-advanced further education, Department of Education and Science. Available from HMSO.

'Safety in school microbiology', *Education in Science*, April 1981, ASE, College Lane, Hatfield, Herts, AL10 9AA.

Technicians Guide to Microbiology, 1981, ASE.

Your local MISAC adviser will offer help and advice on all aspects of work using microbes. MISAC is the Microbiology in Schools Advisory Committee. It has representatives from schools, educational organisations and industry. MISAC aims to help teachers:

- recognise the potential of micro-organisms in teaching,
- recognise the relevance of micro-oganisms to man,
- use micro-organisms safely in the laboratory.

MISAC has a system of local advisers. Please ask your science adviser for details or write to The Secretary, MISAC, Institute of Biology, 28 Queensbury Place, London, SW7.

CHAPTER 1

BIOTECHNOLOGY: AN INTRODUCTION

WHAT IS BIOTECHNOLOGY?

Biology is the study of living things, which are made of *cells*.

A typical cell

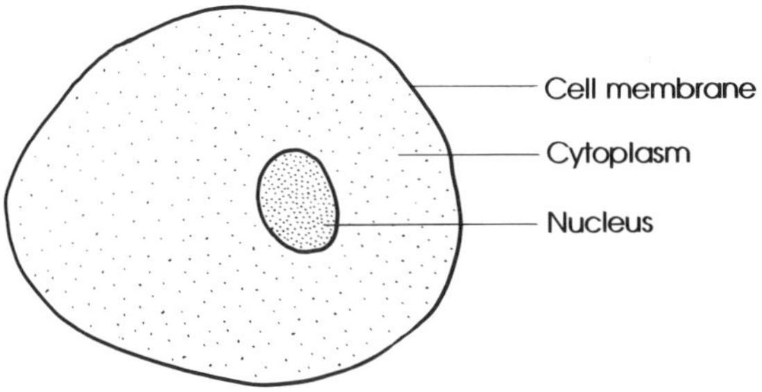

Technology is about solving problems and making things.

Biotechnology uses organisms, cells, or parts of cells, to make and do things we need. These cells may come from microbes, plants or animals.

(a) A bacterium

(b) A mould, or fungus

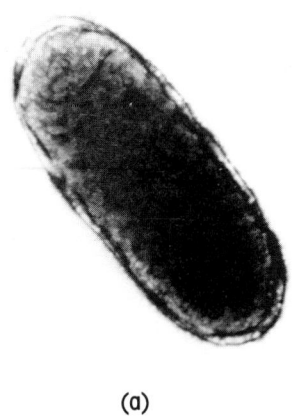

(a)

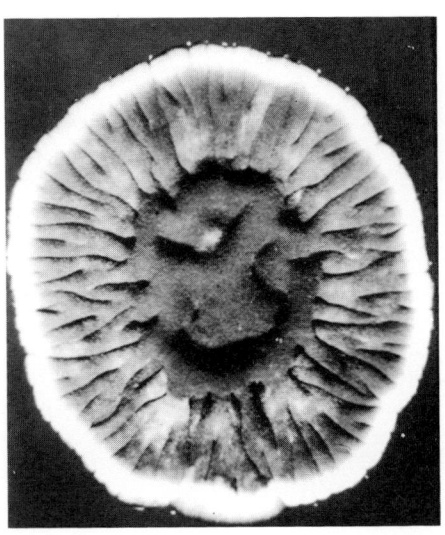

(b)

1

Microbes (micro-organisms) are living things which are so small they can only be seen by using a microscope.

Some people say that biotechnology is the 'factory farming' of cells. More precisely it is the use of biological processes to provide goods and services. These goods include food, fuels, medicines and chemicals.

Waste water treatment and pollution control are services which depend on biotechnology.

The biotechnology tree

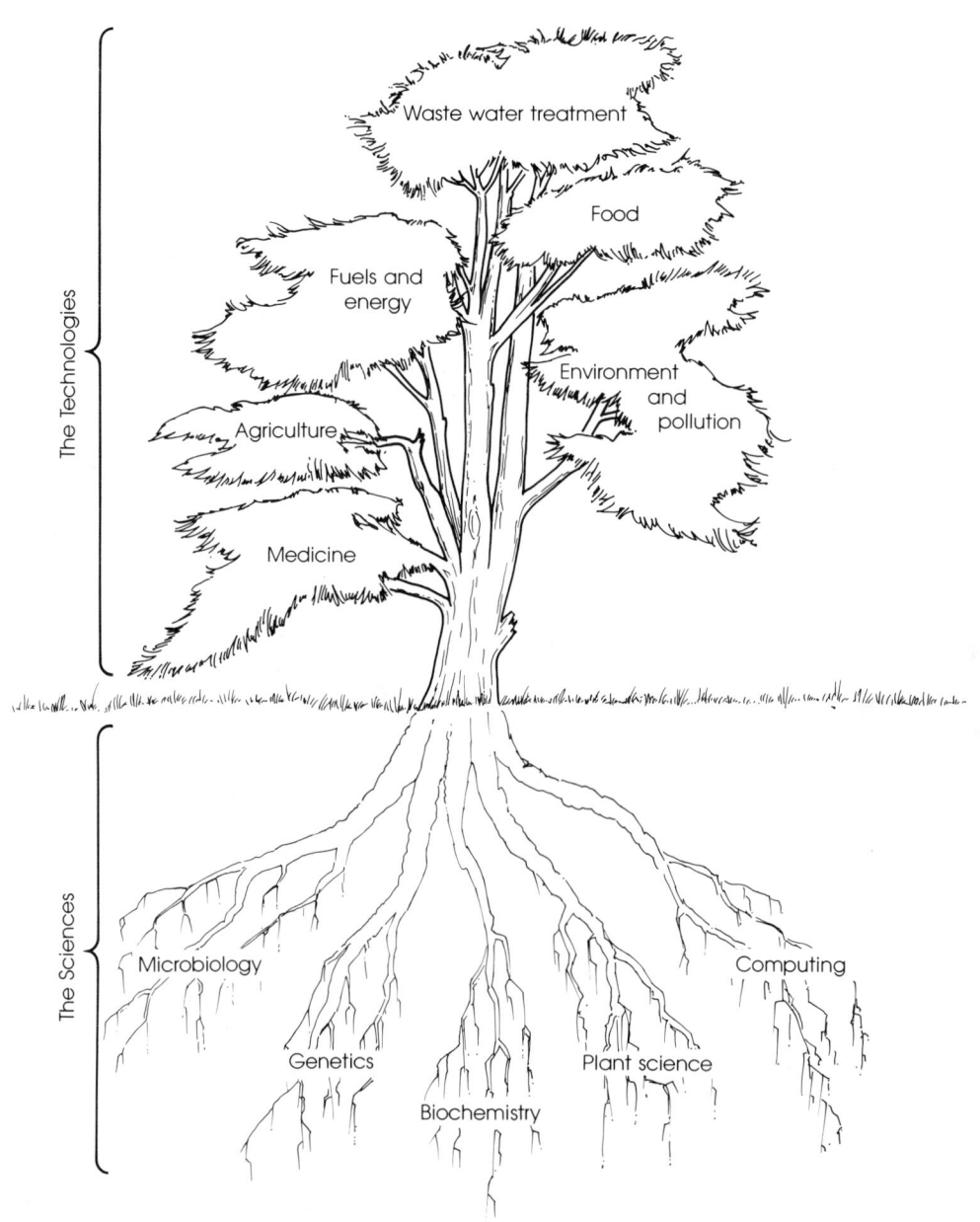

The bio-industries

Type of biologically-based industries	Some products
Agriculture	Animal embryos, compost, pesticides, silage

Chemicals	Acids, enzymes, metals

Energy	Alcohol, biogas, biomass

Food	Dairy products, new foods, sugar syrups, vitamins

Health	Antibiotics, antibodies, vaccines, hormones

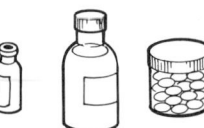

Service industries	Oil recovery, waste management, water purification

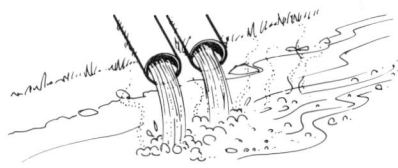

These are the main industries which constitute biotechnology.

Products of traditional biotechnology

A study of biology is important in order to understand aspects of biotechnology. There are many different branches of biology e.g. microbiology, which is the study of microbes.

Branches of biology

Branch	The study of:
Bacteriology	Bacteria
Biochemistry	The chemical reactions which occur inside living things
Botany	Plants
Cytology	Cells
Enzymology	Enzymes (biological catalysts)
Genetics	Heredity – how characteristics are passed on from generation to generation
Molecular biology	The fine detail of cells (at molecule level)
Microbiology	Micro-organisms – these include bacteria and fungi
The bio-industries rely on some or all of these branches of biology, together with other sciences and branches of engineering, which are often under computer control.	

A study of engineering and computing is also important if we are to appreciate what biotechnology is really about.

A definition of biotechnology

'scientific and engineering principles' rely mainly on:
- microbiology
- biochemistry
- genetics
- engineering

'biological agents' include:
- plant cells
- animal cells
- micro-organisms
- enzymes produced by these three groups above

'The application of *scientific and engineering principles* to the processing of materials by *biological agents* to provide *goods and services*' (OECD report, 1982)

'goods and services'
- goods are products of these industries:
  - food
  - drugs
  - chemicals

- services are mainly concerned with:
  - water purification
  - waste management

The engineer provides the surroundings in which the cells work. Typically the cells are placed in a container called a fermenter. This is often under computer control.

Some aspects of biotechnology go beyond the simple definition above. Some recent developments are more like science fiction! For example, animals are being bred which are half one species and half another, such as a half goat, half sheep.

Biotechnology is often computer controlled

CASE STUDY 1

Plant tissue culture and oil-palms

Although plant tissue culture is not a new technique it is only in recent years that it has been applied on a commercial scale. It is now an important area of plant biotechnology. A large company called Unilever began research using oil-palms in the 1960s. Success in this area, with large-scale production, was reported in the early 1980s.

Plant cells may provide useful products such as rubber and drugs. The cultured cells may produce new sources of chemical substances. Also some plants are difficult to grow from seed. This is the case with oil-palm.

In the tropics, where palm trees grow, all parts of the plant are used, providing shelter, fuel, food and drink. Companies like Unilever have grown palm trees for their fruit for a number of years. Oil is squeezed from the fruit to provide products such as margarine, detergents, soap and cooking oil. Tissue culture techniques have successfully been used to increase the yield of oil. Trees selected for growth might not naturally produce offspring with the same high productivity. It is for this reason that tissue culture techniques are used.

Initially, breeding programmes are carried out to produce a parent plant which will yield large quantities of oil. From this parent plant large numbers of identical plants can then be grown by using tissue culture techniques.

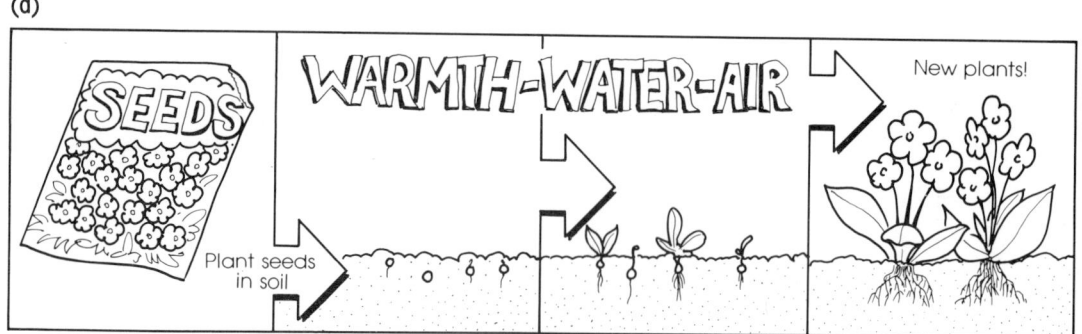

(c)

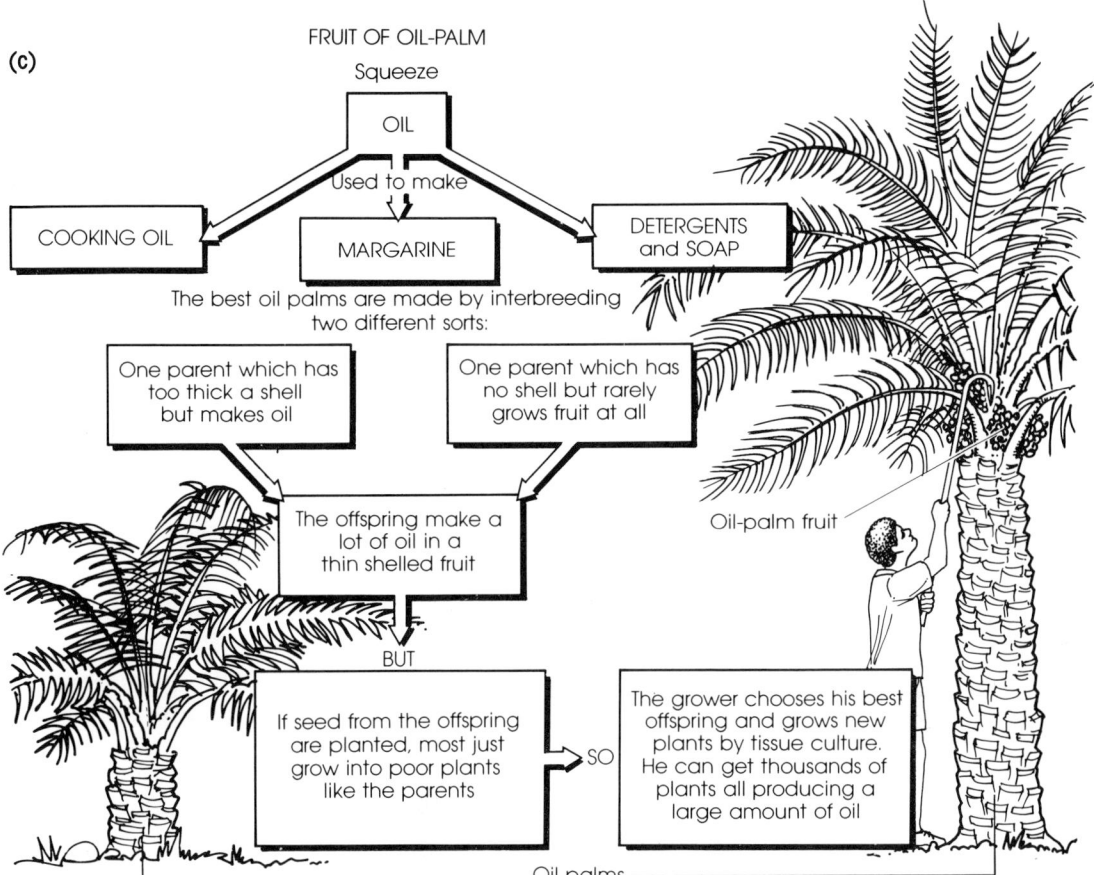

All about tissue culture:
(a) How the gardener grows plants
(b) How to grow plants by tissue culture
(c) An example of the use of tissue culture

The first step is to remove a small part of the growing point from the parent plant. This small part contains only a few cells. It is then grown under artificial conditions on agar jelly in a petri dish. Division of the cells occurs under ideal conditions. For this purpose food, hormones and a suitable temperature are provided. The result is a group of identical cells. If these cells are then separated each will develop, after a time, into a small plant or plantlet. Each of these is identical to the parent plant. These first steps are carried out by Unilever in laboratories in the UK.

The plantlets are then packed and exported to oil-palm plantations in countries like Malaysia. Here the plantlets are grown into individual oil-palm trees. If enough individual cells are cultured originally then large numbers of identical palm trees can be grown.

At this stage the value of tissue culture techniques is limited to those food or ornamental plants where each individual organism is valuable. Plants for food such as raspberries and peaches can be grown using these methods. Orchids and Swiss cheese plants are two examples of decorative plants which can be grown using these techniques.

Stages in tissue culture

However, research is at present being carried out on field crop plants such as corn or wheat. In future it may be possible to change the genetic make-up of these plants by using modern techniques. Large numbers of identical 'modified' plants can then be grown by using tissue culture methods. Science fiction now! Reality later!

CASE STUDY 2

Are extinct animals really extinct?

If you were born one hundred years ago you may have seen a *quagga*. Even then it would have been unlikely as there was only *one* at the time! It was living in a zoo in Holland. Otherwise the quagga was extinct. Like dinosaurs and dodos it had gone for ever. Or had it?

The quagga, now extinct – or is it?

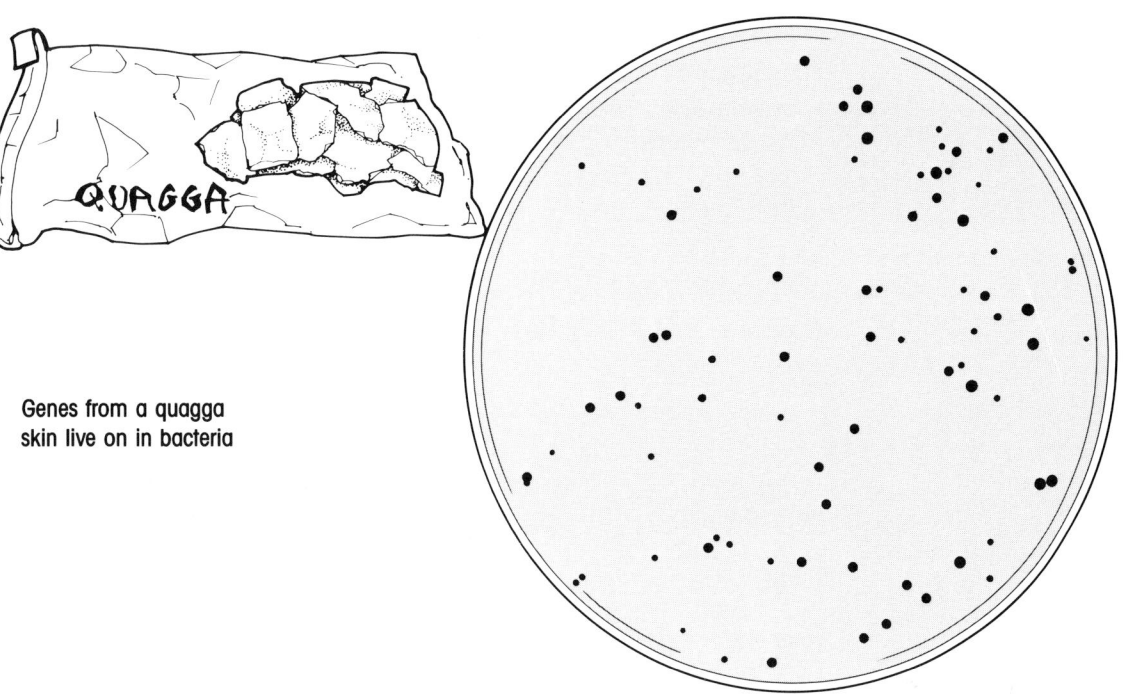

Genes from a quagga skin live on in bacteria

Unlike the others the quagga has *not* gone completely. Its genes live on in microbes like those grown in an ordinary petri dish. Genes are tiny fragments inside cells which carry the blue-print of life.

This is because scientists have recently obtained genes from pieces of dried skin. This had been in a museum for about 150 years. Even so the genes were inserted into microbes which can reproduce strange genes as well as their own.

Genes are made of the chemical *DNA* in which the atoms are arranged in a pattern like a long spiral staircase. The scientists had obtained only a few short pieces of the staircase. The DNA had broken into pieces during its storage in the museum. There was enough material however to confirm that the quagga was a relative of the Mountain Zebra which lives in Africa.

This gives the (faint) hope that the quagga can be reborn. If – and only if – biologists could obtain the correct pieces to produce a complete set of quagga genes this could be possible. Even then they would need to fertilise an egg of a Mountain Zebra, remove the nucleus and then insert the complete set of quagga genes. A test-tube quagga? Fact or fiction? True or false? Possible or not? It *is* possible, but difficult!

Removing the genes of extinct animals has only been carried out recently. Growing these genes inside microbes is one development of genetic engineering. This is the transfer of genes from one organism to another, *of a different kind*.

Genetic engineering, which has developed since the early 1970s, has brought biotechnology to the forefront. Biotechnology promises to produce new foods, drugs and fuels. It promises to bring life from the dead, to prevent extinction! What was once a pipedream promises to be a reality.

The techniques used in genetic engineering have been in use for less than 20 years. However biotechnology has been around much longer than that!

BIOTECHNOLOGY: PAST AND FUTURE

6000–4000 BC: Beer, bread and wine

It can be said that biotechnology started before 6000 BC when Babylonians used yeast to make alcohol in the form of beer.

Much later, about 4000 BC, the Egyptians discovered that yeast caused dough to rise during bread-making. Wine is mentioned in the Old Testament of the Bible, where it says that Noah drank too much!

Some important developments in biotechnology

Traditional biotechnology	Before 6000 BC	Yeasts used to make beer and wine.
	4000 BC (approx)	Yeasts used to make bread.
	Before AD 1500	Algae harvested from lakes as a source of food by the Aztecs.
Scientific biotechnology	1686	Anton van Leeuwenhoeck made the first microscope and discovered microbes.
	1870s	Louis Pasteur indentified microbes as the cause of food and drink going 'off'.
	1890s	Alcohol first used as a fuel in motors.
	1897	Edward Buchner discovered that enzymes from yeast can convert sugar into alcohol.
	1912	Microbes used in large-scale sewage works.
	1912–15	Bacteria used to produce acetone, butanol and glycerol. These are important industrial chemicals.
	1928	Penicillin discovered by Alexander Fleming.
	1944	Large-scale production of penicillin began.
	1953	Crick and Watson discovered the structure of DNA.
	1950s	Many new antibiotics produced.
Modern biotechnology	1973	First genetic engineering experiments.
	1973	New fuel programme using alcohol began in Brazil.
	1976	Guidelines on genetic engineering drawn.
	1982	Human insulin made by microbes.

These are all products of yeast fermentation

Beer, bread and wine-making depend on the fact that yeast cells can live without oxygen. They produce a gas, carbon dioxide, as well as alcohol. This is a process called *fermentation*. Why does beer or wine make people drunk? If you eat lots of bread are you drunk? What happens to the alcohol produced in bread-making?

Other ancient fermentation processes include the growth of acetic acid bacteria to make vinegar. Lactic acid bacteria can preserve milk in the form of *yoghurt*. Many types of bacteria and moulds convert milk to cheese. This traditional biotechnology was used without any real understanding of the processes involved.

17th century: Microbes are identified

In fact microbes provided food and drink for more than 8000 years before they were identified in the 17th century. It was then that Anton van Leeuwenhoeck, using one of the first microscopes, described microbes as tiny **animalcules**.

Many people at the time thought that such living things could grow automatically from non-living things. They thought, for example, that insects came directly from mud. This was called the theory of *spontaneous generation*. Spontaneous means 'immediately', or 'automatically'. Generation, in this case, means 'making living things'.

In the 19th century Louis Pasteur disproved the idea of spontaneous generation and showed that microbes came from pre-existing microbes.

Pasteur, in his laboratory in Paris, studied fermentation

Only microbes can breed microbes. Pasteur developed methods to prevent milk and wine from turning sour. *Pasteurisation* is still in use today.

Some scientists wondered whether the whole microbial cell was needed to make useful products, like alcohol, or whether just parts of it would do.

1890s: Enzymes are discovered

Edward Buchner, in 1897, showed that alcohol can be made by *parts* of cells which contain *enzymes*, rather than whole cells. Enzymes are *biological catalysts*. This means that they are special chemicals made by cells which control the biological activities which we call life.

We are most familiar with the enzymes which help us digest our food. However, enzymes are present inside the cells of all living things. They control all life processes, e.g. nutrition, respiration and growth.

Since 1897 many useful enzymes have been isolated from cells of microbes, plants and animals. They are commonly used in the home and in industry. Enzymes are used in a variety of products, from biological washing powders to chocolate peppermint sweets.

1920s–40s: Penicillin

Penicillin was produced like this in the 1940s

Penicillin is an antibiotic which can help doctors cure many common diseases. It was discovered by Alexander Fleming in 1928 and then made on a large scale during the Second World War (1944). At that time it was considered to be a wonder drug. It certainly saved the lives of many ill and wounded soldiers. Penicillin was made by growing a mould, *Penicillium*, on the surface of a nutrient-rich gel in flat glass flasks. Milk bottles were even used when these flasks were in short supply. It took a lot of time and effort for people to clean and refill these flasks or bottles. The amount of antibiotic produced was small for the workload involved. After the war penicillin was made in larger quantities by growing the mould in a liquid *broth* inside large fermenters.

1953: DNA

In 1953 the nature of DNA was established by scientists working at Cambridge University.

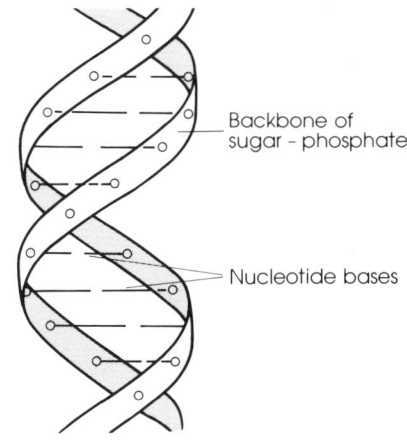

The structure of DNA; the molecule is like a spiral staircase

Each living cell contains a 'little brain' called a *nucleus*. This controls the activities of the cell and is important during cell division. If you look at cells dividing, by using a microscope, long threads, called *chromosomes*, can be seen inside the nucleus. Chromosomes are like a string of beads and are made of units called *genes*. A gene is like one bead in a long string. Each gene controls a particular characteristic of an organism.

Size scale

Dividing cells	Light microscope (× 1000–1500)
Chromosomes within cells	Electron microscope (×1 million)
Genes / DNA within a chromosome	Beyond the microscope

Genes are made of DNA which is the 'blueprint' of life. Genes tell the rest of the cell what to do. They are similar to computer programs in that they contain sets of coded information which tell the cell how to work.

DNA also controls *heredity*. This is the transfer of 'chemical information' from one generation to the next. Understanding the nature of DNA set the scene for genetic engineering.

1970s: Genetic engineering – general outline

Genetic engineering can be used by scientists to 'persuade' microbes and other cells to make products they would not normally make. It can be used to transfer genes, made of DNA, from one type of cell to another *of a completely different type*. This involves high precision work on a very small scale.

Genetic engineering, and some of its other names

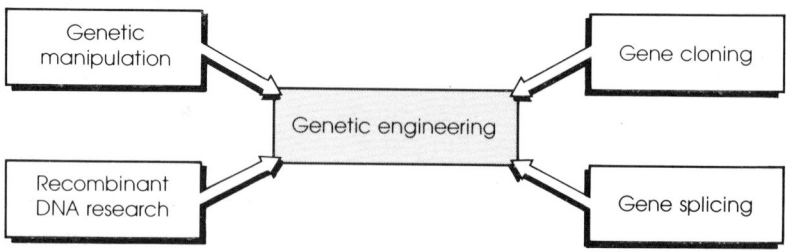

As a result of genetic engineering pieces of genetic material can be taken from different organisms and recombined in ways that do not occur naturally. No extinction? New organisms! What next?!

Genes from humans can be transferred to microbial cells. These human genes cause the microbial cells to make something they would not normally produce in nature. For example microbes can now be persuaded to make *human insulin*. (See page 16, Case study 3)

General outline of genetic engineering

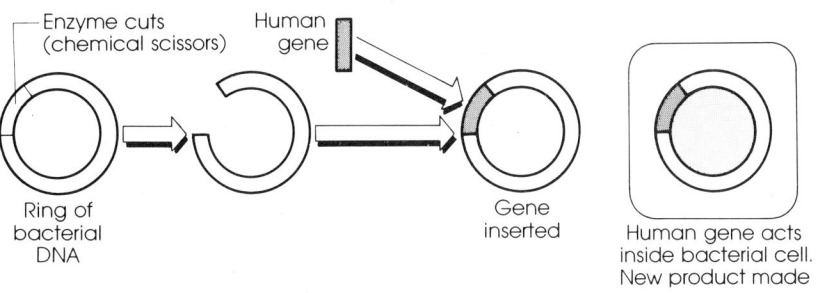

Genetic engineering: a closer look

Before it can be inserted into a microbe, the correct human gene must be obtained. The microbe is then 'persuaded' to make the product, which is collected.

1 Obtaining the correct human gene

The genetic engineer uses test-tubes, glass dishes and special chemicals as tools. These are put to work on the genes of human and microbial cells. The required human gene is identified on the human chromosome so that its position is known. The gene is then obtained by cutting the DNA molecule at certain places using special enzymes as chemical 'scissors'.

2 Inserting the human gene into a microbe

The chromosome of the microbial cell must then be cut by using a similar kind of enzyme. Bacteria, especially a kind called *Escherichia coli* (*E. coli*), are commonly used as the **host** in genetic engineering work. Each bacterial cell has one large circular chromosome, which contains all the genes for its survival. Some bacteria, including *E. coli*, also contain smaller rings of DNA called **plasmids**. The plasmids will often pass from one cell to another.

The human gene is put into a plasmid ring, taken from one bacterial cell. The plasmid's natural ability to enter bacteria can then be used. It carries the human gene into the required microbial cell.

Plasmids also have the ability to make copies of themselves. Once inside the microbial cell they can then multiply rapidly. If the plasmid contains a human gene then that gene is copied. The bacteria (*E. coli*) with the plasmids grow and divide once every twenty minutes or so. Each *daughter cell* so produced receives a few plasmids. Before long millions of offspring are produced from the original bacterium.

A population of cells all obtained from a single ancestor is called a *clone*. All cells in the clone have the same genetic make-up. Therefore within a few days a single bacterium carrying a human gene will yield millions of identical cells. This gene is then said to be *cloned*.

3 Persuading the microbe to start making the desired product

For the biotechnologist it is absolutely essential that the 'foreign' human gene works inside the bacteria. To ensure this a few extra 'tricks' are used. These 'persuade' the bacterial cell to understand the 'language of life' of the human gene it contains. Once the bacterial cell understands the instructions from the human gene it will then start to make the desired product.

Collecting the product

Collecting the product is quite easy, in principle, but expensive to carry out in practice.

The product often remains inside the microbial cells. These lie in a thin 'soup' consisting mainly of water. This water is removed. The product is purified and collected. The whole process is called *downstream processing*.

The new product is now ready for sale.

CASE STUDY 3

Genetic engineering and human insulin production

Insulin is a hormone which is made in a gland, in the abdomen, called the *pancreas*. Hormones are 'chemical messengers' in the body. They control the activity of the body. Insulin regulates the sugar level in our blood. Without enough insulin people cannot control their blood sugar level and suffer from a disease called *diabetes*. People suffering from diabetes (*diabetics*) have to follow a carefully controlled diet. Some also need regular injections of insulin.

Until recently the insulin used to treat diabetics came from the pancreas glands of cattle and pigs. This insulin is not identical to human insulin and may have longterm harmful side-effects. Also the number of people suffering from diabetes is on the increase. It is possible that cattle or pig insulin could not meet the demand from this increased number of diabetics.

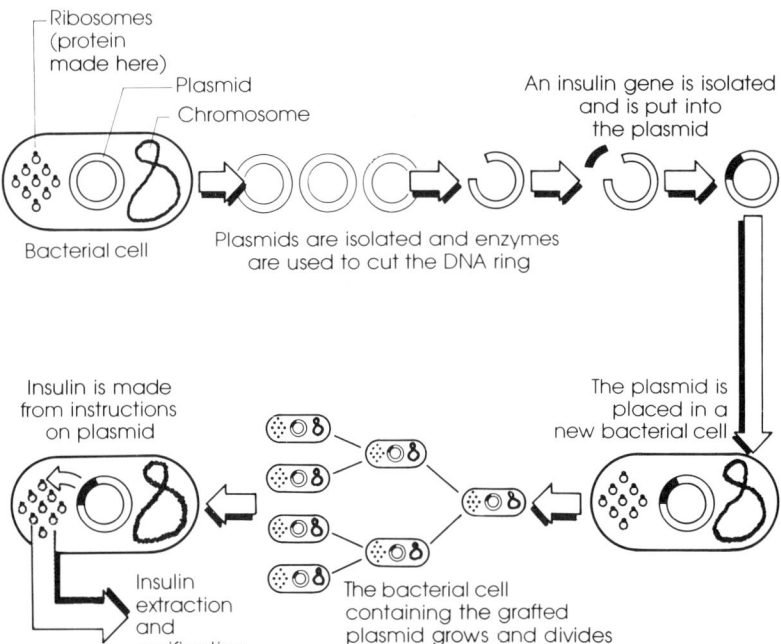

Human insulin can be produced using genetic engineering techniques

Genetic engineering techniques have been used to allow bacteria to produce human insulin. This has been available since the early 1980s. As a result, diabetics now have a good supply of *human* insulin for their injections.

One of the new plants at Speke, near Liverpool, where human insulin is produced

Genetic engineering – why use microbes?

Genetic engineering is now seen as a key tool in biotechnology. It usually involves the transfer of the genes from other cells to microbes. These act as *hosts*.

It is much easier to grow microbes in large quantities than to devise methods of growing plant or animal cells separately in large quantities. Biotechnologists have a great deal of experience of growing microbes on a large scale cheaply and efficiently. This has been done for many years in the brewing and antibiotic industries.

17

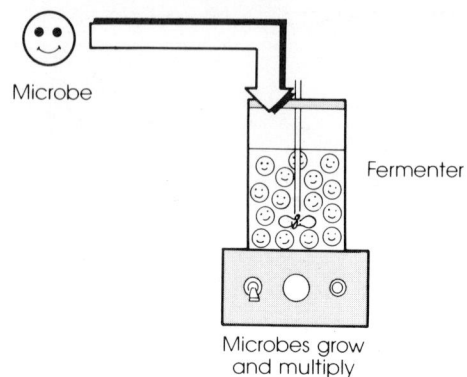

Genetic engineering – why use microbes?

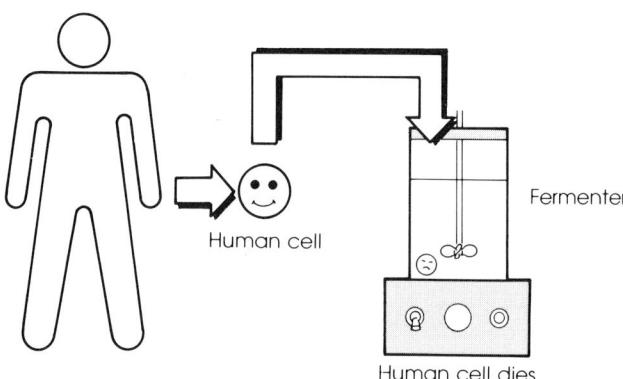

It is very difficult to grow most cells outside their natural environment. However, microbes will grow rapidly under suitable conditions of temperature and food supply. For example, at present it is not possible to grow cells from the human pancreas on a large scale. The pancreas makes insulin which controls blood sugar levels. We have already seen that genetic engineering techniques have been successfully used to create new 'super microbes' which can produce human insulin on a large scale.

Genetic engineering – danger?

With some new techniques, including genetic engineering, scientists can rearrange the basic units of heredity – the genes. When genes are swapped from one organism to another, cells make products they have never made before.

During the 1970s scientists came face to face with the huge dilemma of whether or not to continue with this line of research and the production of new forms of life. They had to balance the possible risks of producing killer 'bugs', which could wipe out mankind, against the possible benefits of producing useful products in large quantities.

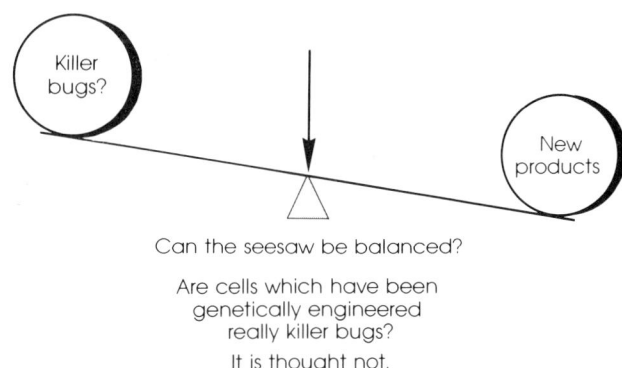

Can the seesaw be balanced?

Are cells which have been genetically engineered really killer bugs?

It is thought not.

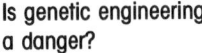

Is genetic engineering a danger?

At one time this became such a cause of worry that scientists who were carrying out some of the first experiments agreed to call a halt to their work. This they did for a period of time until agreed safety precautions were drawn up. In recent years, partly because of the care taken by scientists using genetic engineering, many early fears have subsided.

It is now thought by many that the 'superbugs' constructed by genetic engineering techniques could not survive in nature even if they escaped. They would be unable to compete successfully with naturally occurring microbes.

1970s: other important events – oil

Alongside the advent of genetic engineering, the price of oil increased during the 1970s. What has oil to do with biotechnology? When goods, including fuels, become expensive people look for alternatives. Is there an alternative to oil?

Biotechnology can be used to convert sugars into fuel alcohol. This has replaced petrol for use in cars throughout Brazil.

It is also predicted that fuels such as oil and coal will all be used up during the next century. During *this* century oil and coal have been used as starting materials, in the chemical industry, to make useful products. Biotechnology can also offer alternatives to these chemical processes.

1970s–80s: the biological revolution

Although biotechnology has been with us for thousands of years, only recently has it become a revolution. This has partly been caused by genetic engineering.

For the last 30 years a revolution in chemistry has resulted in the plastics industry. Plastics are now commonplace. Although they can be made from chemicals it is interesting to note that some microbes can also make plastics. Biotechnology offers an alternative.

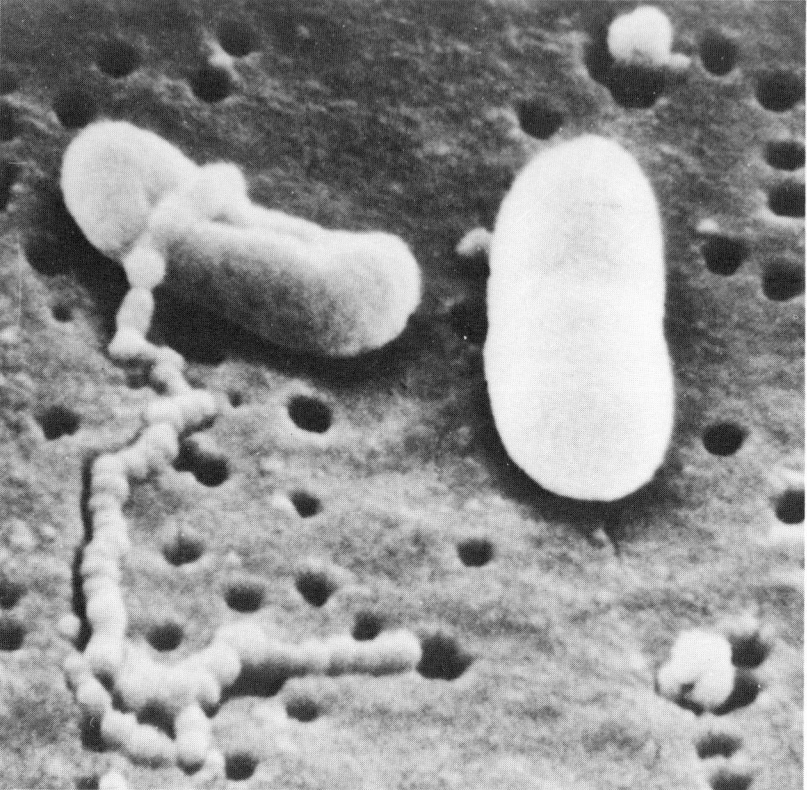

This micrograph shows a whole cell and a damaged cell from which is spilling a polymer chain

Micro-electronics is one aspect of physics. During the last 20 years calculators and computers have been developed as a result of a micro-electronics revolution.

In the last ten years biotechnology has been extending its scope from food and penicillin. It is now also a very important part of the chemical industries.

We are now at the beginning of a biotechnology revolution. This will affect our lives as much as the introduction of plastics and computers.

Biology to biotechnology

Subject	Industry	Time
Physics ⟶	Electronics/computers	20th century
Chemistry ⟶	Plastics	
Biology ⟶	Biotechnology	20th/21st century

1980s and beyond: the biosociety

Many people think that the computer society of today will be joined by the biosociety of tomorrow. Biotechnology will make a major impact on our lives during the next 20 years and beyond. New and improved products which will benefit us all will be created.

But who are biotechnologists?

The people who work in the bio-industries are engineers, microbiologists and biochemists. They work together as a team in an attempt to solve the practical problems which arise in biotechnology.

Who are biotechnologists?

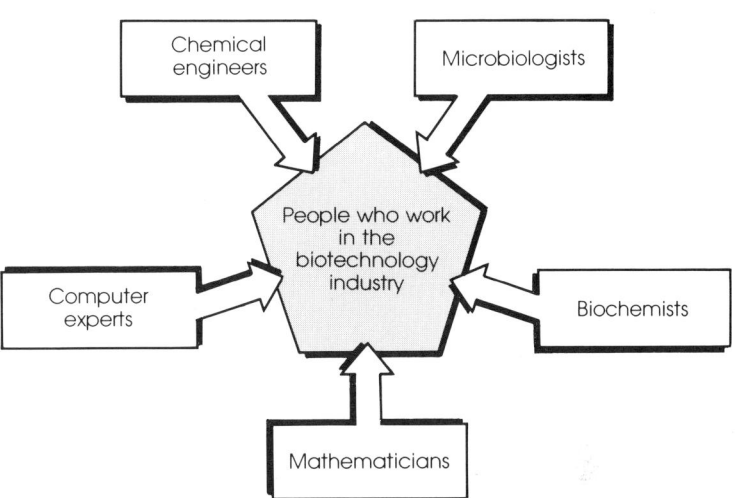

These specialists work together as a team to solve the practical problems which arise in biotechnology

Can biotechnology solve existing worldwide problems, such as disease, famine or pollution? Many people hope so!

In the rest of this book we shall look at some of the ways in which living things work in relation to industrial processes. This will be followed by a more detailed look at the scope of biotechnology. As in this chapter, biotechnological processes are mentioned throughout. Case studies refer to recent examples of biotechnology in action.

SUMMARY

Pieces of DNA called *genes* control the way in which cells work. In biotechnology cells are used as miniature chemical factories. Biotechnologists can modify cells so that they produce large quantities of useful products. A recent technique called *genetic engineering* has meant that not only can cells be modified but new types of cells can be 'tailor-made'. This means that bacteria can now be grown to produce human insulin, for example. Many people think that biotechnology may have a bigger impact on society than computers.

ACTIVITY 1	**Tissue culture of potato plants**

Potato plants are grown commercially by using plant tissue culture techniques similar to the one shown below. Large numbers of identical plants can be grown in a shorter time than when traditional methods of growing potatoes are used. You will need:
- potato
- bunsen
- scalpel
- forceps
- petri dishes containing sterile water (three or four)
- small bottles with cap or cottonwool plug
- growth media* (inside bottle)
- hypochlorite solution/Domestos
- plant pots and potting compost

1) Allow a potato (tuber) to grow shoots.

2) Cut off a piece of potato (2–3 cm by 1 cm by 1 cm) in which there is a bud.

3) Wash in dilute Domestos.

4) Rinse in sterile water.

5) Transfer to sterile growth medium in small bottle. Replace cap.

6) Leave for a period of time (four weeks) in the light at room temperature until plantlet established.

7) Transfer into potting compost inside a plant pot. Keep damp.

Attempt to establish if the following are important. (Change only one condition at a time.)

   (a) The length of tissue in (2). Try 2 cm, 3 cm, 4 cm, 5 cm etc.

   (b) The concentration of Domestos in (3). Try 10%, 20%, 30% etc.

   (c) The number of rinses in (4). Rinse once, twice, three times, four times.

   (d) The position of the tissue in (5), e.g. try upright, upside down, on its side.

   (e) The temperature in (6), e.g. try 15 °C, 20 °C, 25 °C, 30 °C.

   (f) The length of daylight/day in (6), e.g. try 8 hours, 10 hours, 12 hours.

*Murashige and Skoag media – can be obtained from the main school science suppliers.

What are the ideal conditions for tissue culture of potato plants?

How long does it take from the start of the experiment until a potato plant becomes established in (7)?

Try culturing carrot, African Violet and strawberry.

Which tissue works the best – root (tip), shoot (tip), leaf, runner (tip – strawberry only)?

Is this the same for all the different types of plants mentioned?

ACTIVITY 2

What do you know?

Look at the tables and diagrams in this chapter. These should help you to:

- Draw some cartoons to show the main stages in the history of biotechnology, **or**
- Design a poster to show the main industrial areas covered by biotechnology, **or**
- Find out more about (a) bread-making, (b) beer-making, (c) antibiotic production.

QUESTIONS ON CHAPTER 1

1 What is:
   (a) the basic unit of life?
   (b) the study of living organisms?
   (c) the technology based on life processes?

2 Name three branches of biology and briefly say what each branch is about.

3 (a) What are the main stages in tissue culture technique?
   (b) Why are oil-palms grown by using plant tissue culture?
   (c) Name three other plants which can be grown by tissue culture. In each case mention the use of the plant.

4 Is the quagga really extinct? Briefly explain your answer.

5 Which of the following products are made by by using microbes in industry?

   (a) bread   (d) cheese
   (b) beer   (e) yoghurt
   (c) wine

23

6 Why are living cells sometimes called miniature chemical factories?

7 Match the correct letters with the following numbers.
    (i) Pasteur   (a) discovered enzymes.
    (ii) Buchner   (b) discovered microbes.
    (iii) Fleming   (c) disproved the theory of spontaneous generation.
    (iv) Van Leeuwenhoeck (d) discovered penicillin.

8 Starting with the smallest unit write out the following in the correct order of size.
    cell   nucleus   chromosome   gene

9 Why is DNA the blueprint of life?

10 What is genetic engineering? Briefly explain.

11 How do microbes make human insulin?

12 What are the four main stages in genetic engineering?

13 Which two main events/discoveries brought about the recent biological revolution?

14 What types of experts work in biotechnology?

15 Which worldwide problems may be solved by biotechnology?

CHAPTER 2
LIVING THINGS AND INDUSTRIAL PROCESSES

In the bio-industries products such as food and fuels are made by using living cells or parts of cells. But:

- How do cells work?
- What are the important life processes?
- Can cells be grown on a large industrial scale in order to make useful products?
- What is the basic biology on which biotechnology depends?

CELLS AND BASIC BIOLOGY

Cells, DNA and proteins

All life is composed of cells, each of which is a little 'box' in which complex chemical reactions of living things occur.

Each cell contains *DNA*. This controls how a cell works and how it passes on information to new generations of cells. DNA also controls the way in which cell proteins are made.

Proteins and enzymes

Proteins make up much of the structure of cells. However, some special proteins, called *enzymes*, control chemical reactions within cells. They are biological *catalysts*, which alter the rate of reactions inside cells.

What are enzymes?

They are:

- **Proteins.** They are made up of chains of small units called amino acids.
- **Catalysts.** They alter the rate of chemical reactions.

- **Specific.** Each enzyme works best on one substrate only.
- **Efficient.** Each enzyme molecule changes many substrate molecules very quickly.

A *substrate* is a material on which an enzyme works. Specific enzymes act on specific substrates. The enzyme amylase in your mouth acts on starch. The enzyme and substrate fit together exactly, like a key in a lock.

How enzymes work

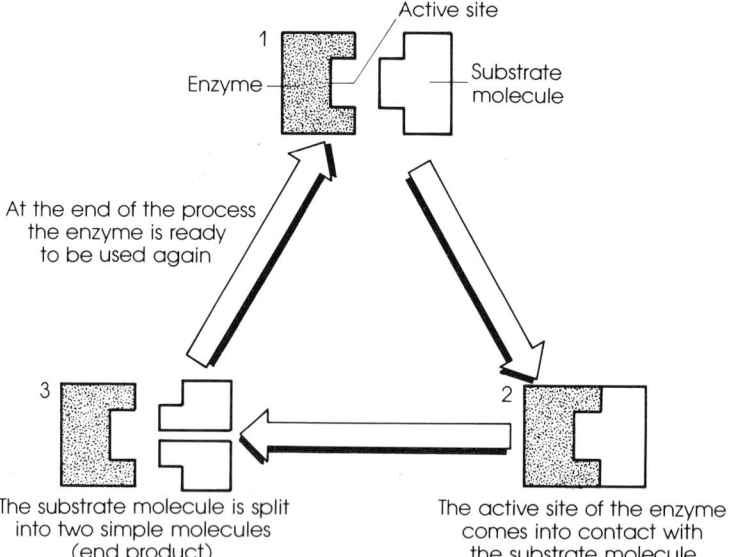

Types of enzyme

We can name three types of enzyme:

- **Amylases** which act on carbohydrates such as starch,
- **Lipases** which act on fats,
- **Proteases** which act on proteins.

Enzymes and catalysts

Catalysts used in the chemical industries work best under conditions of high temperature and pressure. However enzymes, like cells, work best at normal pressure, low temperatures and under neutral conditions.

By *low temperatures* we mean warmth. *Neutral conditions* are those which are neither too acid nor too alkaline.

Let us look more closely at how enzymes work.

HOW ENZYMES WORK

Enzymes and warmth

Enzymes work well in warmth. By that we usually mean in temperatures between 30 °C and 40 °C. Your body temperature is 37 °C, the temperature at which enzymes work best. At low temperatures, e.g. between 0 °C and 10 °C, enzymes work only slowly. As the temperature increases then the rate of enzyme-controlled reactions also increases.

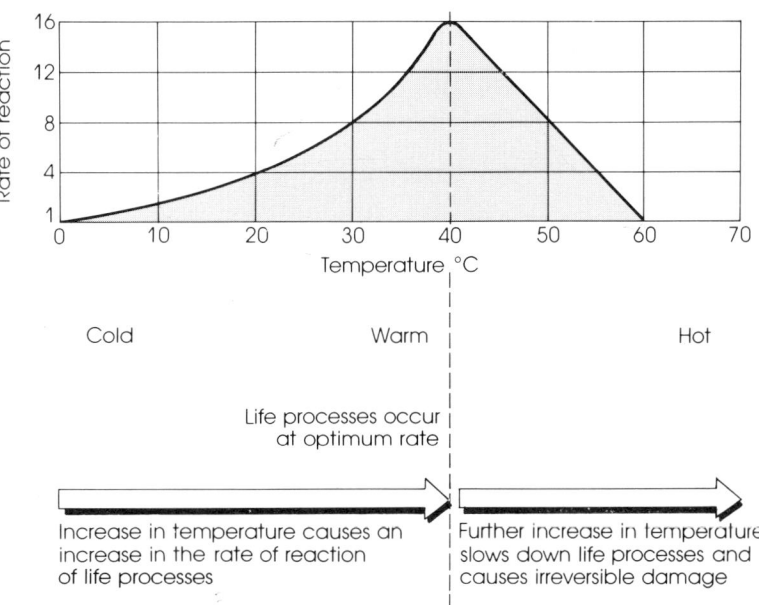

The effect of temperature on enzyme-controlled reactions

In this graph, note that the rate of reaction at 0 °C is 1, at 10 °C is 2 and at 20 °C is 4. At temperatures of 0 °C–40 °C the rate of reaction doubles for every ten degree rise. At 50 °C the rate of reaction slows down. This is because the protein, of which the enzyme is made, is damaged by the high temperature. Very high temperatures permanently damage enzymes.

Uses of enzymes in industry

The following industries use enzymes:

- **Baking.** Enzymes are used to change starch in flour into sugars. Yeast acts on the sugars and causes the dough to rise.
- **Brewing.** Many stages of the brewing process use enzymes. They change starch into sugars (as above), and improve the quality and clarity of beer.
- **Dairy.** Enzymes are used to curdle milk and to prevent cheese from becoming too ripe.

- **Detergent.** Stains, especially protein stains from soil and blood are removed by enzymes.
- **Fruit juice.** Juices are made clear, instead of cloudy, by enzymes.
- **Leather.** Enzymes are used to remove hair from hides and to make the leather soft.
- **Medical.** Enzymes are used to treat disorders e.g. indigestion, to clean wounds and to prepare certain drugs.
- **Textiles.** The preparation of fabrics before weaving uses enzymes.

Warmth and dough

Consider the following examples.

Amylase enzymes cause dough to rise in bread-making.

After dough is made from yeast cells, water, salt and flour it is put in a warm place. Enzymes cause starches in the flour to be broken into sugars. A gas, *carbon dioxide*, is given off which causes the dough to rise.

What happens if you place dough where it is cold? It rises very slowly.

What happens if you then place the same dough in a warm place? It starts to rise quickly.

But what happens if you place the dough where it is very hot? It rises for a while and then stops rising as the enzymes are damaged by the high temperature.

If you then placed the same dough in a warm place would it rise? Why?

Enzymes and neutral conditions

Most enzymes work best under *neutral* conditions i.e. neither *acid* nor *alkaline*. The acidity or alkalinity of a solution can be described by its pH.

pH range

pH describes whether a solution is acid, alkaline or neutral. There is a *pH range* of 1–14.

When the pH is *low* (less than 7) the solution is *acid*. The lower the pH, the more acid the solution will be. Your stomach contents have a pH of 2.

At pH 7 a solution is said to be *neutral*. The contents of most cells have a pH of 7 and so are neutral.

When the pH is *high* (greater than 7) the solution is *alkaline*. The higher the pH, the more alkaline the solution.

The pH scale

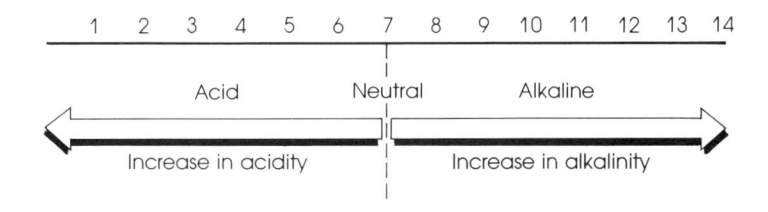

```
    1  2  3  4  5  6  7  8  9  10 11 12 13 14
          Acid      Neutral    Alkaline
    ←─────────────────|───────────────────→
       Increase in acidity    Increase in alkalinity
```

All enzymes work best within very narrow pH limits.

Enzyme A works best at a pH of 2 and would probably be found in the stomach of mammals for example. Enzyme B works best at a pH of 7 and is typical of most enzymes. If you placed enzyme B in a solution which has a pH of 2 would it work? Why?

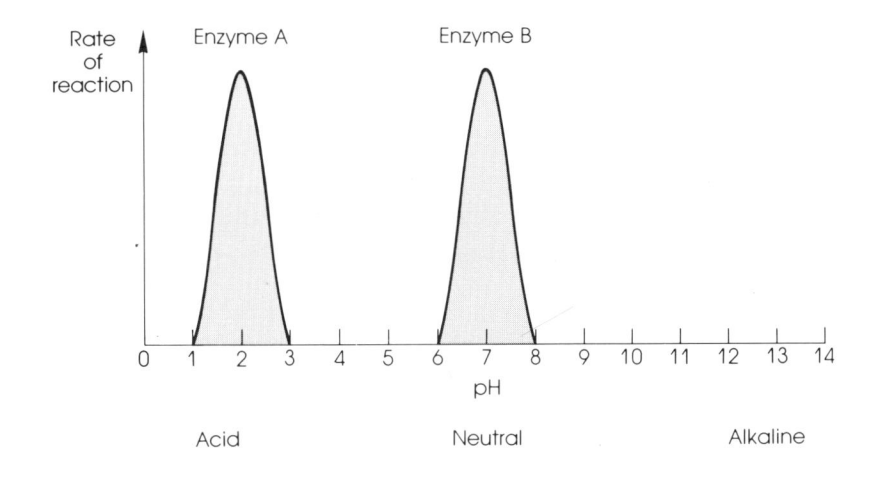

The effect of pH on enzyme-controlled reactions

(Graph showing Rate of reaction vs pH, with Enzyme A peaking at pH 2 and Enzyme B peaking at pH 7. pH scale from 0 to 14, labelled Acid, Neutral, Alkaline.)

CASE STUDY 4

Enzymes, immobilisation and high fructose syrup

Cultured cells containing enzymes may be used to bring about a chemical change. In brewing, for example, yeast cells growing in a sugary solution called *malt* produce beer containing alcohol. The beer is a more expensive product than the sugary starting materials. The chemical change is brought about by enzymes inside the yeast cells.

Traditionally at the end of each production the yeast cells and their enzymes are thrown away. New enzymes or cells are needed for further chemical change. This is inconvenient and costly. Recently techniques have been developed to *immobilise* cells and enzymes. This is explained on the next page. Immobilised enzyme processes have been particularly successful in the production of sugar syrups, e.g. high fructose corn syrup.

Typically, sugars taste sweet. *Sucrose* is probably the sugar you use most. You may put it into your tea or coffee. It is obtained from sugar cane or sugar beet.

Fructose is a similar sugar found in fruits and honey. The production of fructose in the biotechnology industry is a fairly recent event. Fructose has received attention because it is cheaper and twice as sweet as sucrose. It is also more suitable for diabetics.

Whereas in 1970 fructose was not in general use as a sweetener it now accounts for 20% of sweetener consumption in the USA. This is mainly due to two types of enzymes. One group of enzymes, *amylases*, converts cheap starches to glucose. Another type, *glucose isomerase*, converts glucose to fructose. Cheap starch can now be converted, in two stages, into fructose, which is more expensive.

$$\text{Starch} \xrightarrow{\text{amylases}} \text{Glucose} \xrightarrow{\text{glucose isomerase}} \text{Fructose}$$

Enzymes are generally expensive materials. In the example given amylases are relatively cheap but glucose isomerase is expensive. Enzymes need to be used as efficiently as possible, especially for large-scale industrial processes. Enzymes also have the ability to do the same job over and over again.

Glucose isomerase will convert glucose molecules to fructose molecules providing that glucose is available. Under normal circumstances fructose and the enzyme are both dissolved in the final mixture. It is therefore difficult and expensive to extract the enzyme and re-use it with a fresh quantity of glucose.

In recent years this waste of expensive glucose isomerase has been avoided by *fixing* the enzyme on a solid surface. The enzyme is attached to inert materials such as plastic or glass beads in a tube. In industry this is a large tube, called a *reactor vessel*. The enzyme is then said to be *immobilised*.

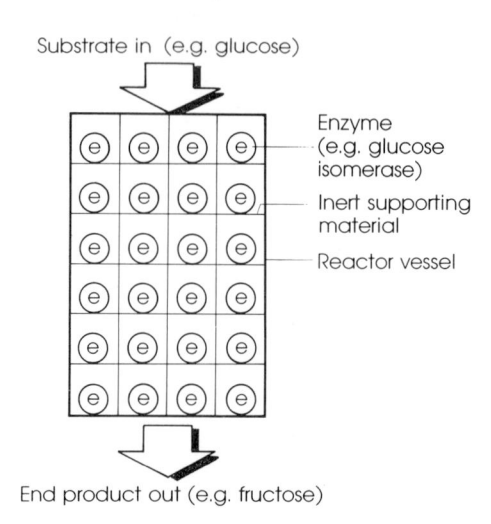

Enzyme immobilisation

Glucose solution is poured into the tube and, as it passes over the enzyme, is converted into fructose, which drains away. The glucose solution is referred to as a *substrate*, or *nutrient medium*, as the enzyme feeds on it. The enzyme remains attached to the beads inside the reactor vessel, ready for further use. Enzyme immobilisation holds many exciting possibilities in the biotechnology industries.

Cells as chemical factories

We have looked briefly at enzymes as the basic functional units within the cell. Biotechnology depends on enzymes and cells, which work as miniature chemical factories. In order to remain alive and work well most cells need *food* and *oxygen* as well as water.

CELLS AND FOOD

The biotechnology industries are based on different forms of life. Many of these are microscopic and include algae, fungi, bacteria and single-celled animals called *protozoa*. These different types obtain their food in different ways. They have different methods of feeding. Whatever the exact method of feeding the following simple facts apply:

- Animal cells cannot make their own food.
- Some plant cells can make their own food.
- Animal cells depend on plant cells, either directly or indirectly, for their food.

Algae are plant cells which include seaweeds and types which form green 'slime' on stagnant water.

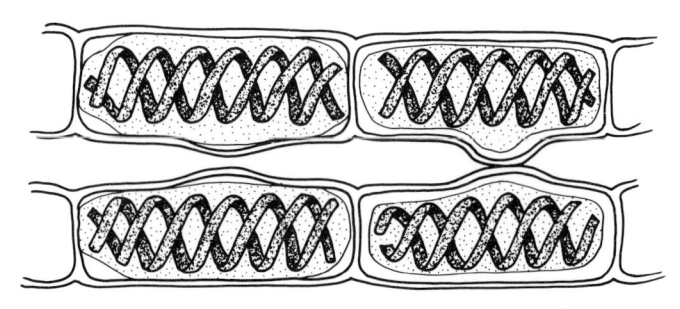

Cells of *Spirogyra* – an alga

Like all green plants and some bacteria, algae can make their own food. They do so by using sunlight energy to join together carbon dioxide and water. This process is called *photosynthesis* and as well as making food, such as starch, bubbles of a gas, oxygen, are given off as a by-product. If you look closely at a stagnant pool, ditch or canal, especially on a hot summer day, you will see bubbles of oxygen around the slimy algal cells.

Fungi cannot make their own food. Plants such as moulds or mushrooms lack the green pigment *chlorophyll*, which is needed to trap sunlight energy during photosynthesis. Some fungi cause *decay* by living on the dead remains of plants and animals. They are called *saprophytes*. Some bacteria feed in the same way. As a result of decay dead bodies of plants and animals are broken down and vital *minerals* are returned to the soil to be re-used in nature.

Not all fungi feed in this way. Other fungi and some bacteria live on or inside the bodies of plants and animals. They 'cheat' by obtaining digested food directly from the plant or animal; by doing this they sometimes cause damage or disease.

Fungi and bacteria which feed like this are said to be *parasites*. They live on or in another organism called the *host*. The parasite gains food and other benefits. The host, sometimes a human, may be damaged. *Fungal parasites* cause diseases such as thrush, athletes foot and ringworm. *Bacterial parasites* cause diseases such as pneumonia and whooping cough.

Most protozoa cannot make their own food and need a ready-made food supply. Protozoa play an important part, by feeding on raw sewage, in waste treatment.

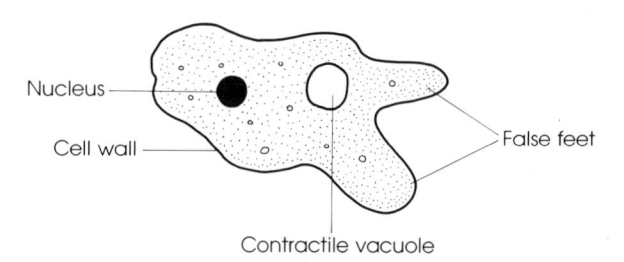

Amoeba – a protozoan

Nucleus
Cell wall
False feet
Contractile vacuole

Generally speaking, however, it is those organisms which feed as saprophytes which are important to the bio-industries, although some which photosynthesise, such as algae, are also important.

CELLS AND OXYGEN

All living things must change food which they have made or obtained into *energy*. Food is sometimes referred to as a *fuel* for life processes. When a fuel is burnt energy is released at high temperatures. However food is 'burnt' at low temperatures (30 °C to 40 °C) in a process called *respiration*. As well as energy, carbon dioxide gas is produced as a *waste product* of respiration.

To respire, most living cells need *oxygen*. This oxygen is in the air and is used by humans and many other forms of life to convert food into energy. Without oxygen most living things cannot respire. However, some living organisms *can* respire without oxygen. *Yeasts* are a good example. In beer and wine production they respire without oxygen and convert food into *alcohol*. The gas carbon dioxide, which makes the beer and wine fizzy, is also given off.

So far we have the cells with their enzymes, which need a supply of food and oxygen in order to grow. In biotechnology the cells and/or enzymes convert raw materials into useful products.

Biotechnology depends on research in the laboratory. Experiments are carried out in test tubes or small containers, but before cells are grown on a large scale inside massive *fermenters*, industrialists carry out tests in a *pilot plant*.

A laboratory fermenter in use

CELLS AND INDUSTRIAL PROCESSES

Scaling up

Progression from small-scale experiments to large-scale industrial processes is called *scaling up*. Experiments which work well in a test-tube may not work in a large fermenter. There are many problems to overcome. Industrialists do not go to the trouble and expense of building a large fermenter before carrying out trials on a pilot plant. This is a *mini fermenter* and is the first stage of the scaling-up process.

Pilot plants

Industrialists need ideal conditions for growing cells on a large scale. These may be easy to provide in a test-tube, but less easy in a tank with a capacity of about 5000 litres. Warmth, food and oxygen must be supplied in a safe and economic manner. pH and contamination must be monitored and controlled. Everything must be *clean* and *sterile*. All of the cells must have ideal conditions for growth.

Engineers build a pilot plant, which may have a capacity of about 100 litres, in order to test conditions and overcome any problems which may develop. Why do they do this? One reason is that large-scale fermenters are very expensive. Problems which may develop may be difficult, if not impossible, to solve unless tests and trials have been carried out in a pilot plant.

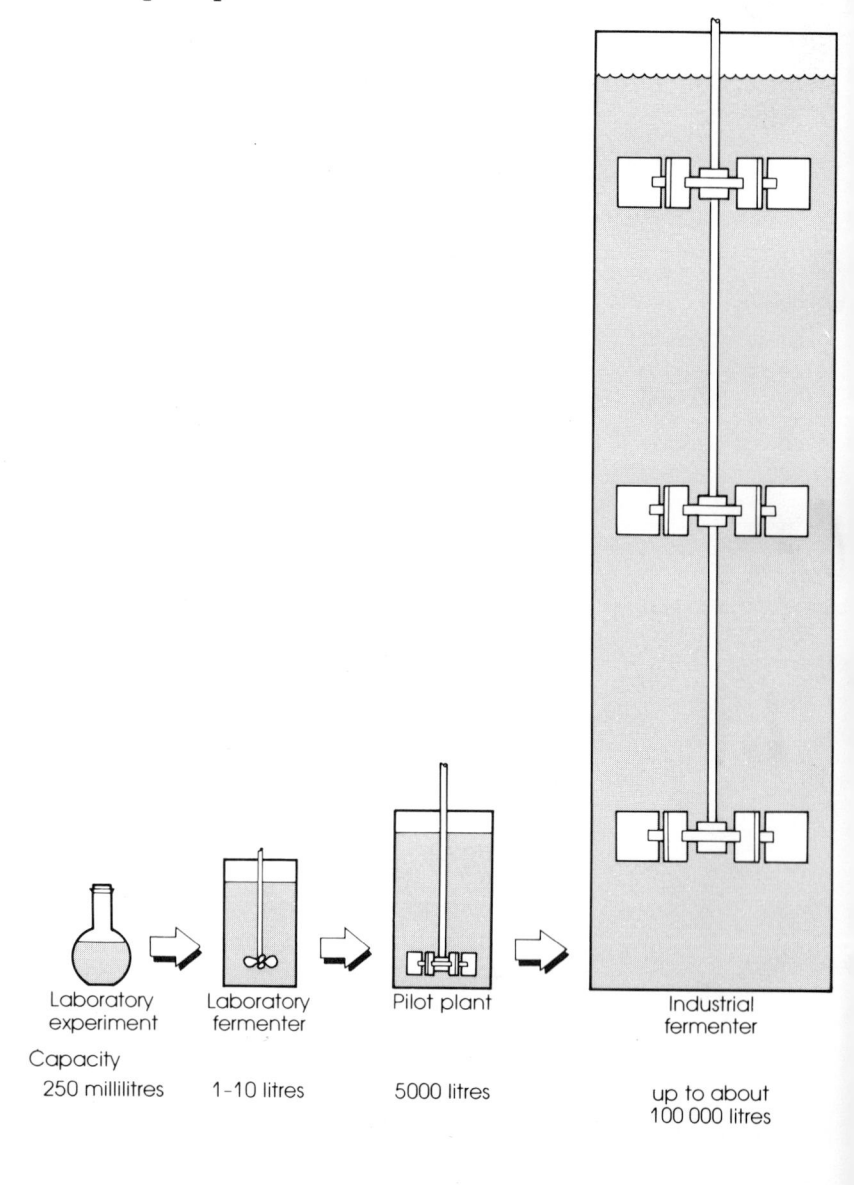

Scaling up

Laboratory experiment	Laboratory fermenter	Pilot plant	Industrial fermenter
Capacity 250 millilitres	1–10 litres	5000 litres	up to about 100 000 litres

34

(a) A pilot plant

(b) Protein plant at ICI, Billingham, UK

Fermenters

A fermenter is a container inside which microbes can be grown. Industrial fermenters are often as large as a block of flats. They have many pipes and valves and are usually made of stainless steel.

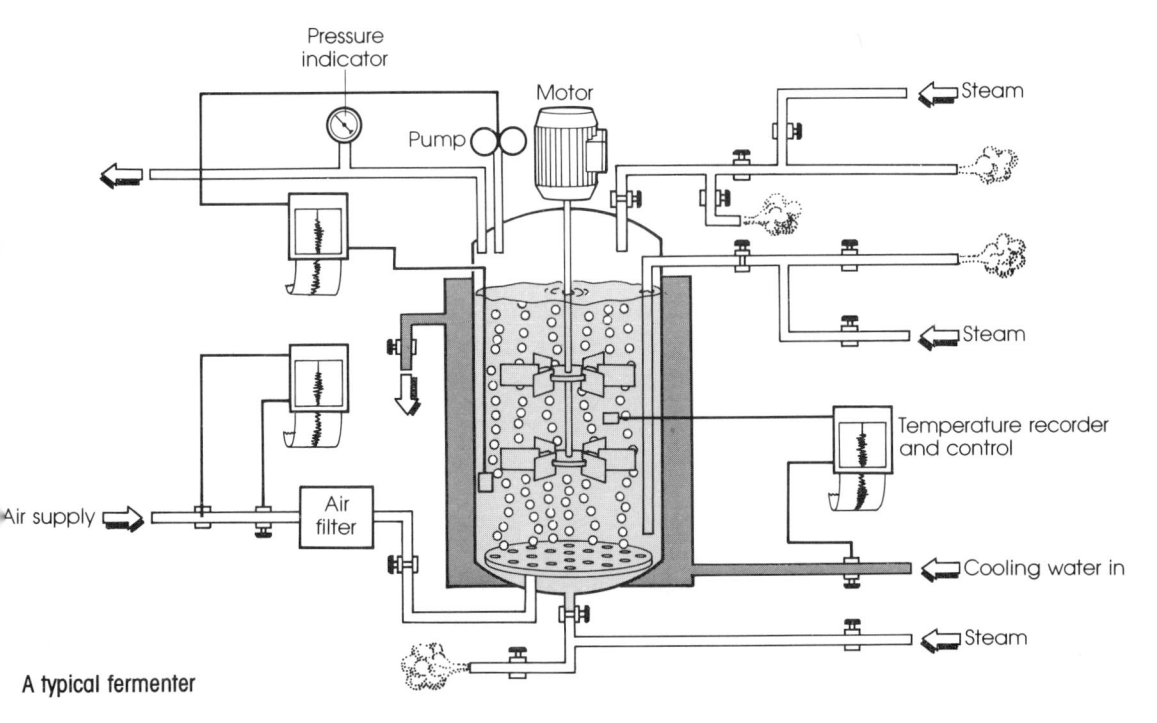

A typical fermenter

35

Some fermenters use *support-growth* systems. This means that cells are grown as a layer on the surface which is in contact with the food supply. This happens when you grow microbes in a petri dish containing *jelly-agar* in the school laboratory. This method was originally used in penicillin production and is still in use in the manufacture of citric acid, which is added to soft drinks.

Most fermenters, however, use *suspended growth* systems. In this case the microbes are suspended in a liquid medium. This is similar to growing microbes in tubes of liquid broth in the school laboratory. This system has been in operation in beer-making for a long time.

The contents of a fermenter must be mixed so that all of the cells have a plentiful supply of food and oxygen.

How fermenters work
(a) Mechanical stirring
(b) Air-lift

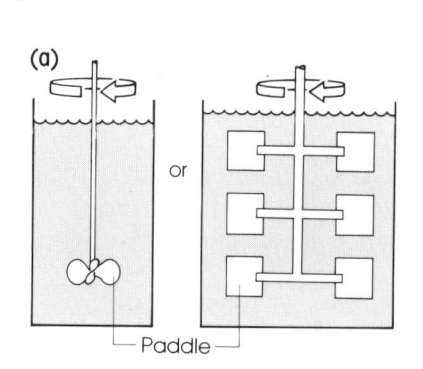

(a) Paddle

The paddles turn and mix the contents

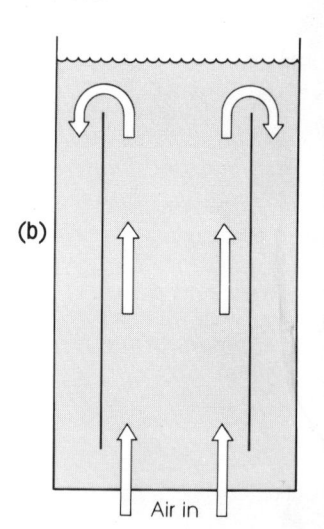

(b) Air in

Air movement and fermenter design cause the contents to mix

Batch fermenters

Traditionally beer was made by running a fermenter as a batch system. The fermenter is filled with foods and microbes and suitable conditions for microbial growth are maintained. After a period of operation the fermenter is emptied and cleaned. The *product* (beer, for example) is purified and the whole process is repeated to make another batch.

Continuous fermenters

Nowadays, batch systems have mostly been replaced by continuous fermenters. The fermenter is filled with the correct foods (*nutrients*) and microbes. Suitable conditions of warmth, oxygen supply and pH are maintained so that the microbes grow well. The end product, together with any wastes, is continuously removed and fresh nutrients automatically enter the fermenter.

The quantity of fresh nutrients continually added is similar to the quantity of products which are continually removed. The result is that once the operation has been started it can run non-stop for long periods of time, perhaps up to six months. Continuous fermenters, although more complex to develop and run, are much more efficient than batch fermentation systems.

The work of biotechnologists

A team of expert biologists and engineers work together to:

- choose suitable cells to grow,
- decide on the correct raw materials needed for growth,
- design and operate a fermenter,
- sterilise equipment and raw materials,
- control growth rates,
- control product recovery.

SUMMARY

In biotechnology living cells are used in industrial processes to convert raw materials into useful products.

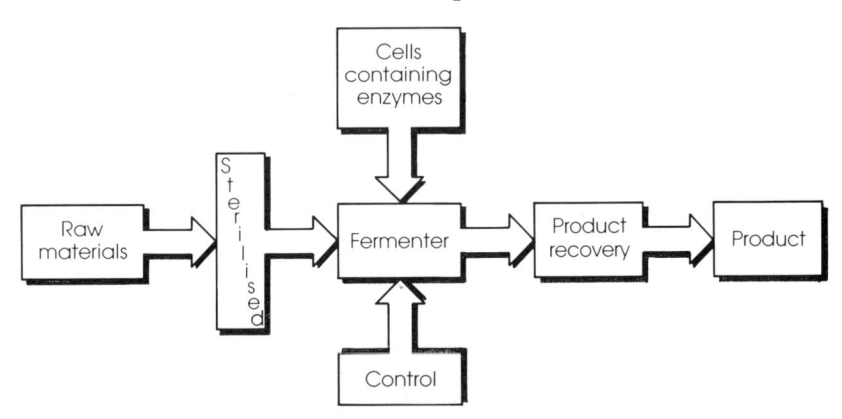

The main stages in a typical biotechnology industry. The raw materials, cells and fermenter are all sterilised

In order to increase efficiency, ideal conditions for growth must exist. These include warmth, a suitable pH and a food supply. Oxygen may also be necessary.

The living cells may grow well inside small containers in the laboratory, but in large-scale industrial production certain problems have to be overcome. It is not easy for engineers to design fermenters which will provide ideal conditions for all of the cells they contain. Before these large fermenters are developed trials are carried out in a pilot plant. This is a smaller, less expensive fermenter which provides conditions similar to those to be used during actual production.

Definitions

Raw materials Cheap starting materials which will be converted into a useful product by the living cells.

Sterilise To clean thoroughly. This prevents contamination or growth of other organisms which will affect the product made.

Cells The living thing consists of cells which are controlled by enzymes. An enzyme is the functional unit of a cell.

Fermenter The container inside which the cells grow.

Control Nowadays computer control of fermenters automatically provides ideal conditions for the growth of cells. Computers control the movement of valves and pumps in the fermenter.

Product recovery Cells grow in a dilute solution inside the fermenter. In order to recover the useful product it must be purified. Quite often large quantities of water and other materials are removed. Product recovery is sometimes called downstream processing.

Product This is the material which is made and sold.

ACTIVITY 3

Experiments with washing powders

Soap powders such as Lux do not contain enzymes. Some washing powders, such as Ariel, contain enzymes and are said to be *biological* washing powders.

Do soap powder and biological washing powder both work as well

- on all types of stain?
- at different temperatures?

Use the same type of material e.g. white cotton, for each experiment.

1) Cut the sample of material into six pieces, then stain two pieces with soil, two with egg, two with grass. Make up solutions with the soap powder and the biological washing powder – using the same concentration – and put three pieces of material – one soil stained, one egg stained and one grass stained – in each solution.
Examine at five minute intervals, up to half an hour. Which type of powder works better?

Try your own experiments. Use different types of washing powders or different stains, but only vary one factor at a time; e.g. if you compare one biological washing powder with another, test at the same temperature on the same type of stain on the same material.

2) For one of the materials in (1) above compare the action of soap powder with biological washing powder on material soaked for 15 minutes in water at
   (a)   15 °C (cold water from tap),
   (b)   40 °C (warm water),
   (c)   100 °C (boiling or very hot water. **Care!**)
   Does biological washing powder work well in hot water? Why?

QUESTIONS ON CHAPTER 2

1 What is a cell?

2 Why is DNA important?

3 Briefly describe what enzymes are and how they work.

4 What is 'enzyme immobilisation'?

5 How do each of the following groups of microbes obtain their food?
   (a)   Algae
   (b)   Fungi
   (c)   Protozoa

6 What is 'respiration' and why is it important?

7 Why is a 'pilot plant' developed as part of the 'scaling-up' process?

8 What is a fermenter? Briefly explain the difference between:
   (a)   support-growth systems and suspended growth systems,
   (b)   batch fermenters and continuous fermenters.

9 Look back at the summary on p. 37. Suggest which stages in a typical biotechnology industry may be expensive to operate. Try to explain why.

CROSSWORD ON LIVING THINGS AND INDUSTRIAL PROCESSES

First trace this grid on to a piece of paper (or photocopy this page – teachers please see note at the front of the book). Then fill in the answers. Do not write on this page.

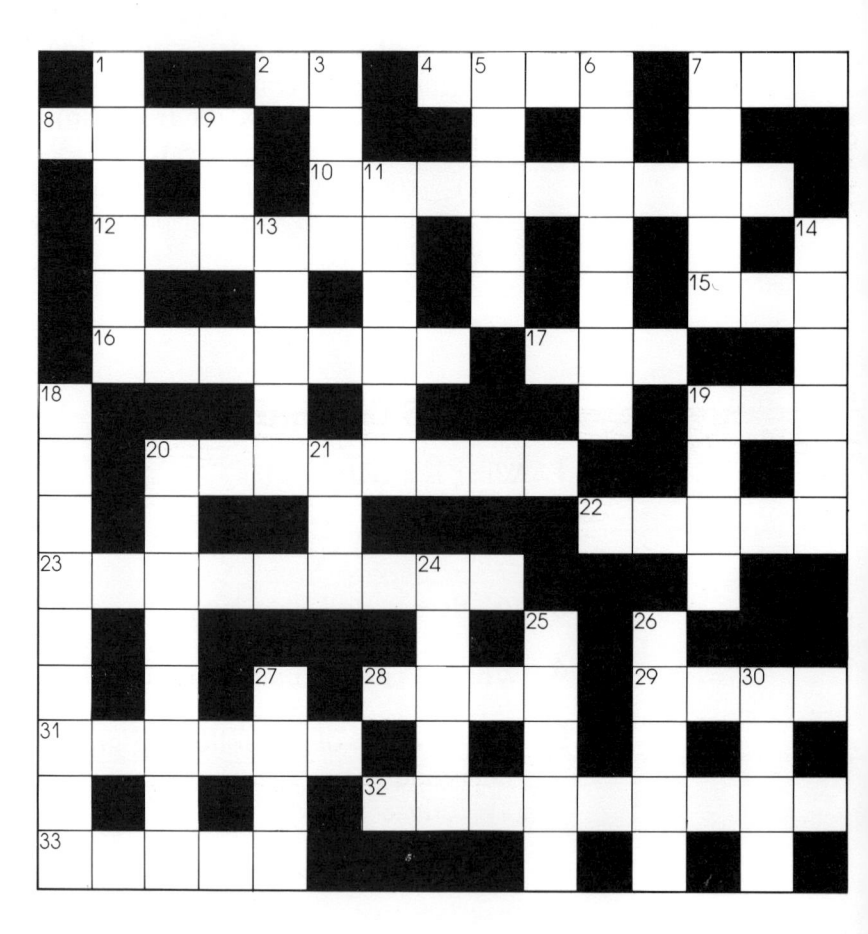

Across

2 Measure of acidity and alkalinity (2)
4 A layer of dirt on top of water (4)
7 The thread of life (3)
8 Not entrance (4)
10 Progression from laboratory experiments to industrial processes (7, 2)
12 Makes things bigger or taller (6)
15 Not cold (3)
16 Neither acid nor alkali (6)
17 Neither solid nor liquid (3)
19 ___ of chocolate (for example) (3)
20 Lives on a host (8)
22 A fermentation process which is not continuous (5)
23 An enzyme which changes glucose to fructose (9)
28 Jelly – food for microbes (4)
29 ___ or death (4)
31 Special type of protein which controls chemical reactions within cells (6)
32 These (see 31 across) act on proteins (9)
33 Begin (5)

Down

1. A gas in the air (6)
3. Holds a party – or a parasite? (4)
5. Units of life (5)
6. Animal, vegetable or ___? (7)
7. Bread before it is baked (5)
9. More than one! (3)
11. What a parasite does (6)
13. A common liquid! (5)
14. Amylases act on ___ (6)
18. Skilled craftsmen who make things work (9)
19. ___ or shower? (4)
20. Single-celled animals (8)
21. We breathe ___ (3)
24. Sucrose is a ___ (5)
25. Liquid food for microbes (5)
26. Simple water plants (5)
27. To give out (4)
30. Coal, gas or oil (4)

CHAPTER 3

BIOTECHNOLOGY AND FOOD

Good food is needed for good health. While many of us have plenty of food there are millions of people in the world today who are starving. Traditionally food has been produced by farming. Crops are grown and livestock is reared. The first applications of biotechnology however were in food production.

Centuries ago Mexican Indians harvested algae as food and people in the Middle East made bread, beer and wine. The greatest impact of biotechnology so far has been in the *food processing industry*. Food from farming, such as milk, is *processed* or changed by biotechnology, into another food type, such as cheese.

Modern and future applications of biotechnology promise more food which is cheaper but has a high nutritional value. Much of this food, derived from microbes, plants or animals, will benefit both well-fed and starving people of the world.

MICROBES AND FOOD PROCESSING

In simple terms food processing means changing food when it is being prepared. Most foods are changed during preparation, as cooking is a type of processing. However many examples exist in biotechnology where microbes are used in food processing.

Type of food	*Processed by microbes to make*
milk	cheese
milk	yoghurt
barley	beer
grapes	wine
wheat	bread
vegetables	pickle

TRADITIONAL INDUSTRIES

The ploughman's lunch

A ploughman's lunch consists of cheese and pickles, with bread, washed down with beer. These are all products of traditional bio-industries.

Making cheese

Milk is needed to make cheese. It is heated or *pasteurised* to kill any harmful bacteria which may be present. The pasteurised milk is then poured into large containers where it cools to about 30 °C. *Starter* is then added to the milk. This contains special bacteria grown under carefully-controlled conditions. These bacteria make the milk thicken and turn sour, as an acid is made in the process. *Rennet* is then added to the souring milk. Traditionally rennet was obtained from the stomachs of young calves. Nowadays rennet may be 'artificially' produced by microbes. Rennet contains an enzyme which causes lumps or *curds* to form in the milk. A watery liquid, called *whey*, is also formed.

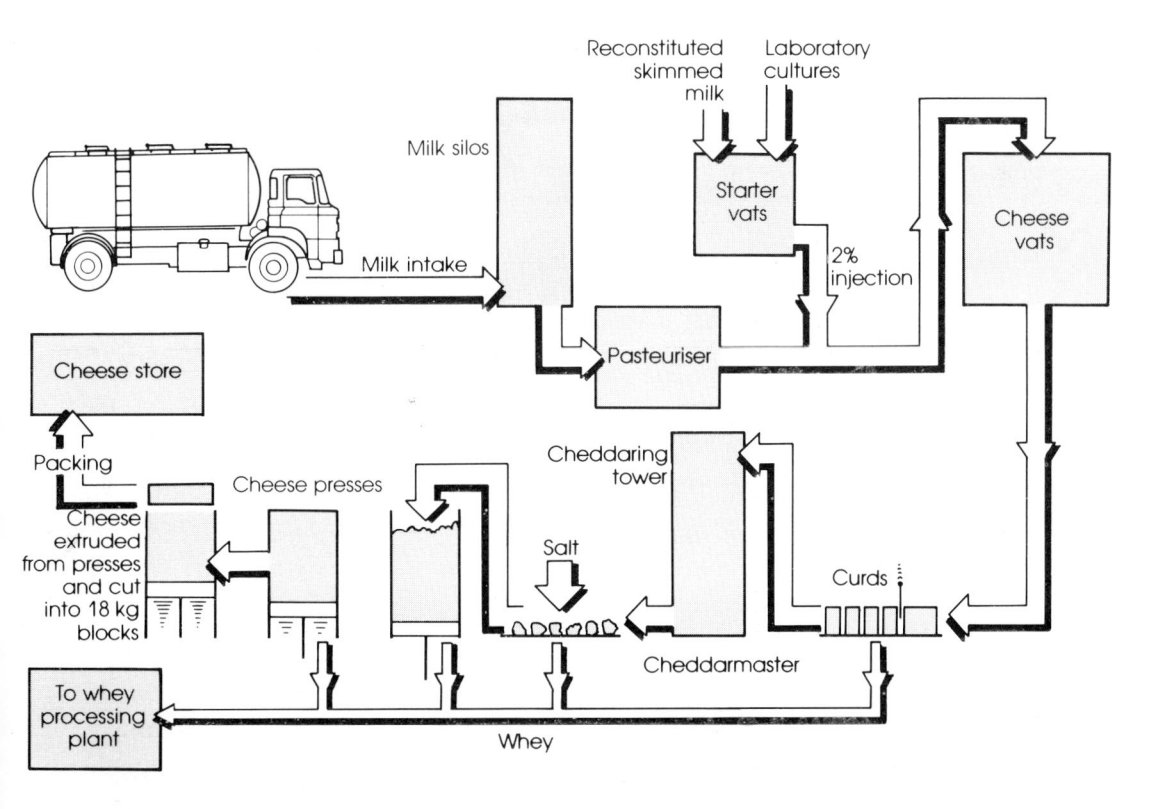

A flow diagram showing cheese production

The whey is drained away. It is not used in cheese-making, but contains protein and may be used as an animal feed. After salt is added to the remaining curds they are squeezed to remove further liquid and placed into moulds. Then they are stored in a cool place to mature and ripen to form cheese.

Different types of cheese are made by using variations of the above method.

In the cheese-making process, heat-treated milk is pumped into large vats. Starter is added and the milk is turned into curds and whey by the rennet

Some, or all, of the following will affect cheese production:

Starter
The type of starter used will determine the type of cheese made. Most starters contain bacteria of the *Lactobacillus* type.

Liquid removal
Soft cheeses are squeezed less and contain more liquid, like cheese spreads. Hard cheese, such as Cheddar, have most of their liquid removed.

Length of ripening
Young cheeses, such as cottage cheese, are not left to ripen. Some cheeses, such as Stilton, are left for a much longer period of time for the mature quality to develop.

Additional processes
Some cheeses, such as Danish Blue, have an extra strong flavour as blue fungi are encouraged to grow inside the cheese.

Making bread

Two important ingredients of bread are *flour* and *yeast*. Flour is made from wheat grains which have been ground up. Yeast is a microbe which causes the bread to rise. A dough is formed by mixing together flour, salt, yeast and water. After kneading, the dough is left in a warm place to rise. It does so because yeast cells *ferment* or *respire* and produce the gas carbon dioxide. This makes the dough light and fluffy.

The sugar for the fermentation comes from the flour. Enzymes called *amylases* in the flour change starches into sugars. In some flours – e.g. those from North America – not enough enzyme is present. Extra fungal amylase is added to break down some of the starch into sugar.

After being shaped and placed into moulds the bread is baked in an oven.

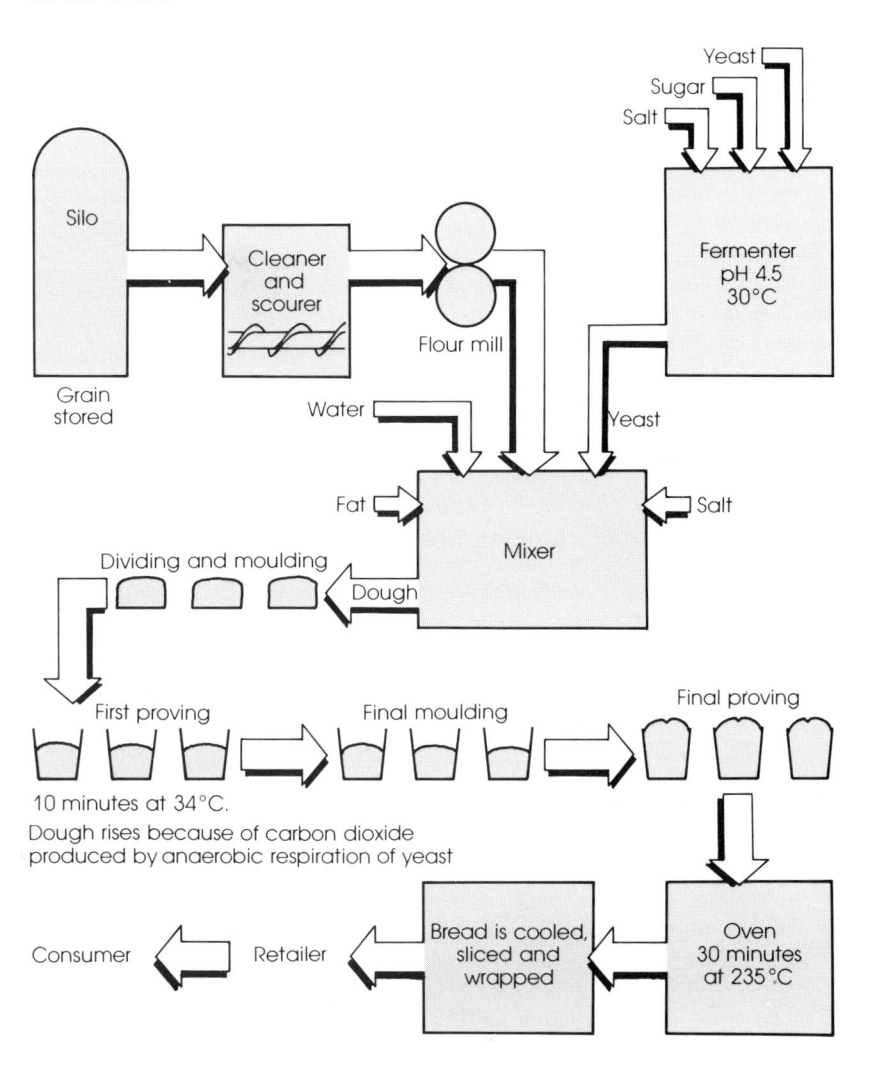

Bread-making

Making vinegar

Pickles are vegetables, such as onions, preserved in vinegar. In Britain most vinegar is made from 'young' beer. The beer is allowed to trickle down tall towers packed with wood shavings. On the shavings grow *Acetobacter* bacteria. After about five days these bacteria convert the beer to vinegar. This collects at the base of the tower. It is then tapped off to be bottled or used to make pickles.

45

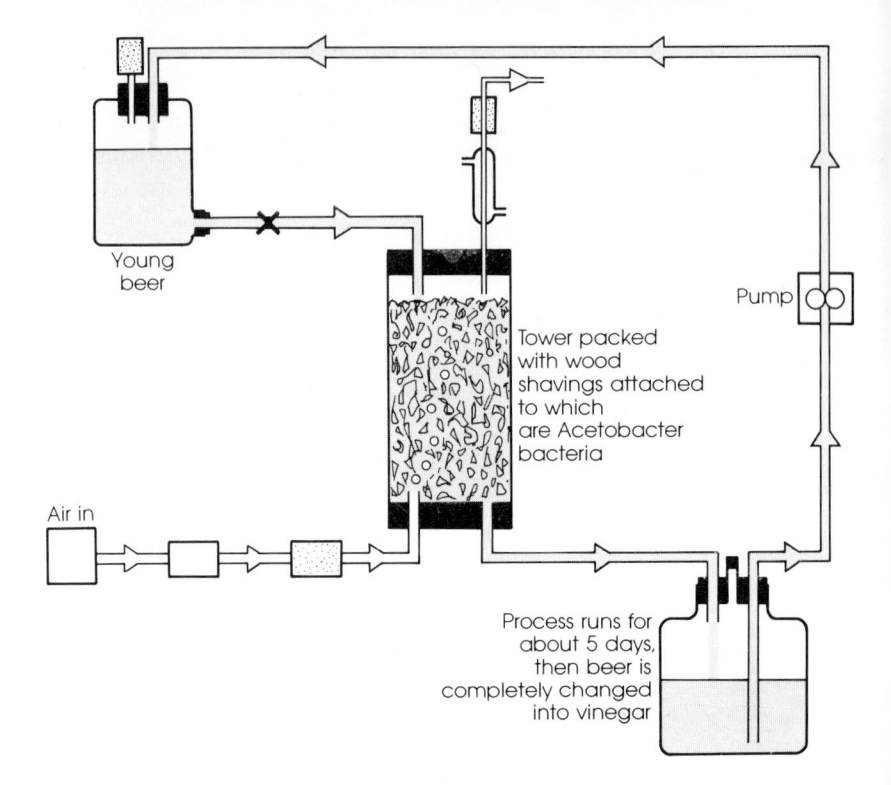

How vinegar is produced from 'young' beer

Young beer

Tower packed with wood shavings attached to which are Acetobacter bacteria

Pump

Air in

Process runs for about 5 days, then beer is completely changed into vinegar

Making beer

As well as yeast, *barley*, another type of cereal, is used in beer-making. Barley grains are left to germinate in warm, damp conditions. During the process starch is broken down into sugars by enzymes within the grains. Malted barley or *malt* is formed. This is crushed and mixed with warm water. It is allowed to stand for a few hours, during which time the

Fermentation of beer

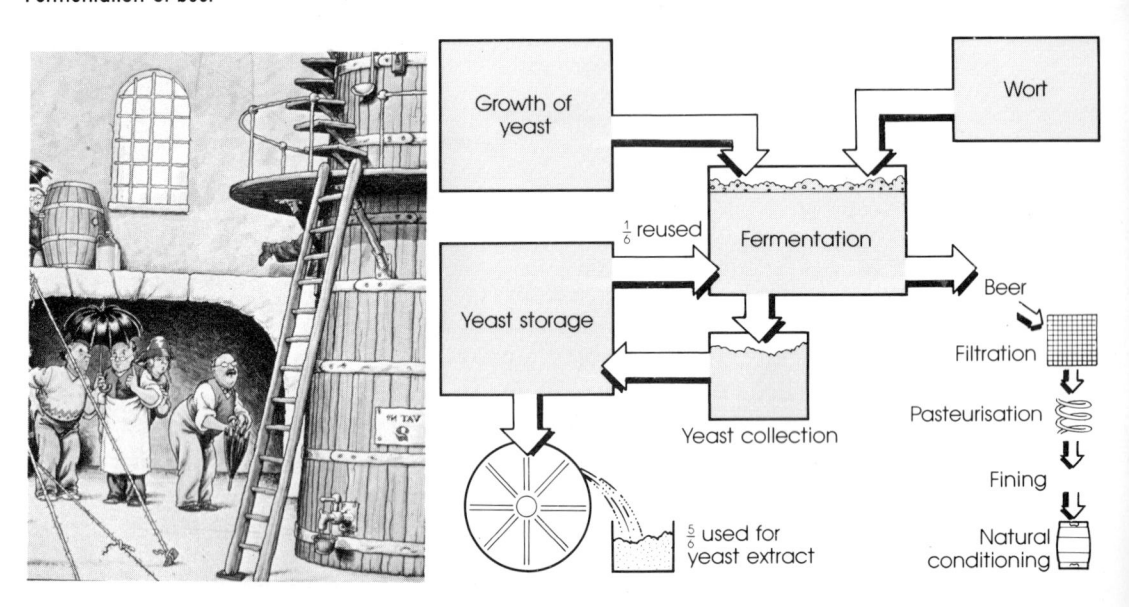

Growth of yeast

Wort

$\frac{1}{6}$ reused

Fermentation

Yeast storage

Beer

Filtration

Yeast collection

Pasteurisation

Fining

$\frac{5}{6}$ used for yeast extract

Natural conditioning

46

enzymes continue to break down starches into sugars. After being filtered the mixture is called *wort*. This is boiled with sugar and hops, which give flavour to the beer. Boiling destroys the enzymes so that no more malt is made. After cooling the liquid is poured into a large stainless steel fermentation vessel, where yeast is added. This *ferments* or *respires* and turns the sugars from malt into alcohol. The mixture is again filtered, before storage, during which time it matures.

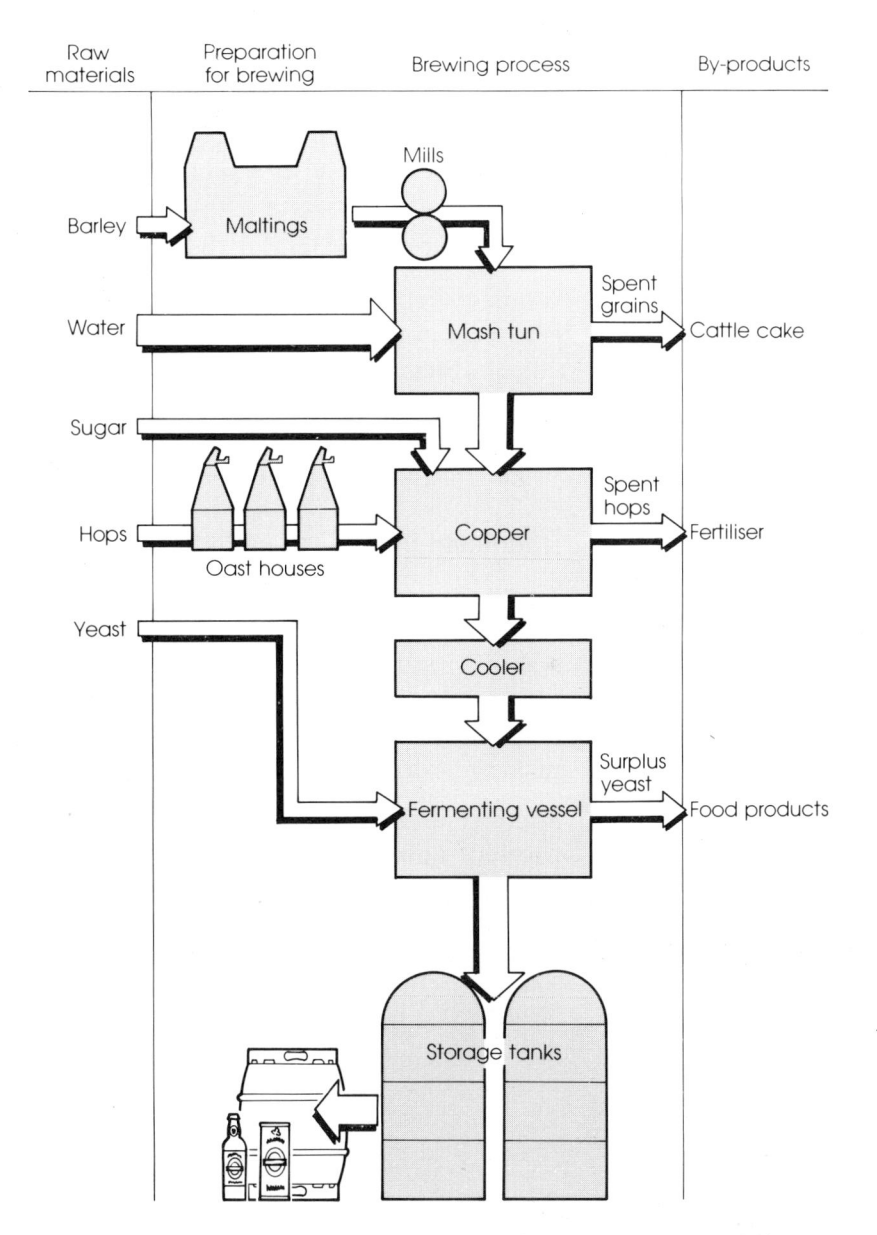

Brewing beer

Raw materials	Preparation for brewing	Brewing process	By-products
Barley	Maltings → Mills	Mash tun	Spent grains → Cattle cake
Water			
Sugar		Copper	Spent hops → Fertiliser
Hops	Oast houses		
Yeast		Cooler	
		Fermenting vessel	Surplus yeast → Food products
		Storage tanks	

Cheese, bread and beer are traditional examples of foods which can be made by using microbes during their preparation. Another traditional product is yoghurt.

Making yoghurt

In industry partially skimmed milk is used for yoghurt manufacture. It is thickened slightly and pasteurised to kill harmful bacteria.

After being warmed in large tanks a bacterial 'starter' is added. This starter consists of two different kinds of bacteria. These are *Streptococcus themophilus* and *Lactobacillus bulgaricus*. The two types of bacteria act together to cause the milk to thicken and go sour. The temperature is important, for the optimum growth temperatures of the two bacteria differ slightly.

Ideally a temperature of about 40 °C is maintained so that *both* bacteria can act on lactose sugar in the milk. This is changed into lactic acid which gives the yoghurt its flavour. As more acid is produced the mixture clots and thickens.

When the correct level of acidity, taste and consistency is reached the yoghurt is cooled. This slows down the activity of the 'starter' bacteria. These bacteria do remain alive in the yoghurt however. It is therefore advisable to store yoghurt in a cool place to prevent the production of too much acid.

Traditional industries, modern technology and new products

These traditional industries *have* been affected by modern technology. Advances in enzyme technology and genetic engineering have resulted in the faster production of high quality products. A good example of this is a type of Japanese beer. It is made in one day. Traditionally the complete beer-making process took weeks.

Some traditional processes have been slightly modified to produce new products.

CASE STUDY 5

What's English, soft, blue and new?

Lymeswold is a new cheese. It is a mild blue, soft cheese, which is similar in appearance to Brie or Camembert. It has a creamy texture and a white mould crust. Like Stilton and Danish Blue, Lymeswold contains blue veins, but the veins are lighter and the cheese has a milder flavour.

Lymeswold came on to the market in the early 1980s. The company making the cheese identified the soft continental type as a good product. This was because the number of households buying this type of cheese had risen by 50% in recent years.

This new cheese is made in Somerset, England. It is made in a similar way to Brie. Starter and microbial rennet are added, which causes the milk to thicken. It is cut to release curds and whey, and ladled into perforated moulds to drain.

After being washed in salt solution and pierced to allow blue veins to develop, the cheese is left to ripen. During this process it is exposed to an atmosphere containing white mould spores. These help form the crust. After two weeks the cheese is sufficiently firm to cut and wrap. It is then left to ripen for another fortnight, before being sold.

The general trend nowadays, however, is to use microbes directly as a source of food.

CASE STUDY 6

Algae as food

Algae are simple plants that live in water. Many algae are rich in proteins, minerals and vitamins and therefore may be suitable as food. Many hundreds of years ago Mexican Indians collected the alga *Spirulina* from lakes where it grew. It was then dried in the sun to provide a protein-rich food with a mild taste. Much interest is now being shown in growing algae such as *Spirulina* as a source of food. In some hot countries algae are cultivated in artificial ponds, which are

Spirulina is cultivated in artificial ponds in Israel

easy and cheap to make. Algae can make their own food by photosynthesis (see p. 31). They grow rapidly and give very high yields when compared with other food sources.

Type of organism	Yield of protein (kg/hectare)
beef cattle	100
wheat	4000
spirulina	50 000

In hot countries and desert areas farms of the future may not grow traditional crops. They may consist of rows of polythene-filled ponds or tunnels containing *Spirulina*. The algal cells, after harvesting and drying, make a protein-rich food. Air and light are free and only a few cheap chemicals need be added to maintain high productivity.

CASE STUDY 7

Fungi as food

We have traditionally eaten fungi, such as *mushrooms*, but can we be persuaded to eat other types of fungi which are rich in protein? One such fungus is a mould called *Fusarium*. It contains about 45% protein, which compares favourably with meat. It also has a high fibre content. Fibre is an important part of the diet, as it adds bulk to food and helps intestinal muscles to work efficiently. A British company, RHM, has developed a method of growing *mycoprotein* (protein from fungus). *Fusarium* grows well on a variety of waste starches from wheat or potatoes, for example. The fungus can then be used to make artificial meat by adding appropriate flavourings. It has a texture which is chewy and similar to meat. If it were put into beefburgers, some people may find it difficult to tell the difference between *real* beef and *fungal* beef!

Making mycoprotein

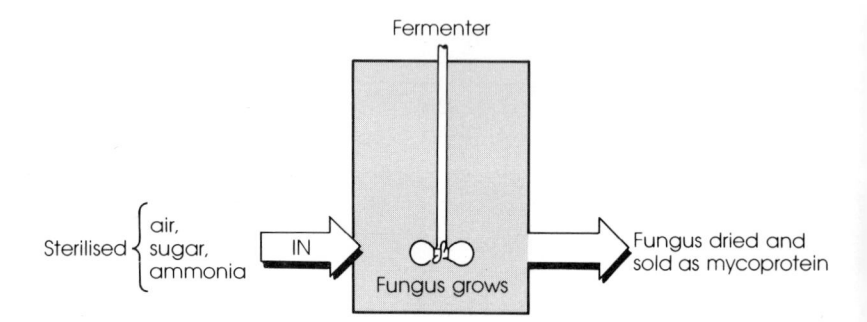

CASE STUDY 8

Bacteria as food

A number of companies have developed methods of growing bacteria as a protein-rich food. Perhaps the most successful venture has been that of ICI with their production of *Pruteen*. Research and development was lengthy and expensive. Fifteen years after initial work was started the Pruteen plant became fully operational in the early 1980s.

The type of bacterium which they grow is called *Methylophilus methylotrophus*. This grows well on *methanol*, a chemical made from North Sea gas. For rapid growth these bacteria need some mineral salts, ammonia and air, as well as a suitable temperature and pH. To maintain an efficient process sterile conditions must be present. One advantage of using methanol is that very few other microbes will grow in it. This means that the chances of contamination are very small.

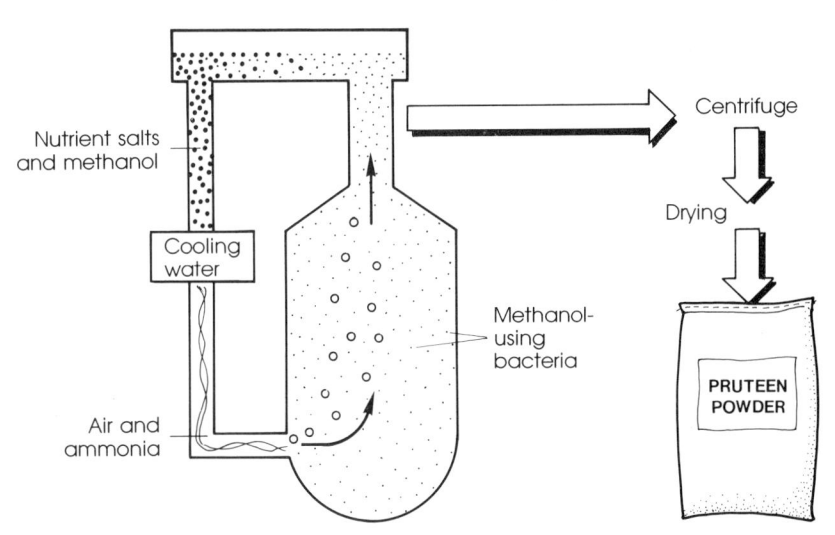

The pressure cycle process for growth of bacteria on methanol

ICI developed a large-scale continuous culture technique in Pruteen manufacture. Once the process is started up, some of the bacterial cells are continually removed and replaced with a similar quantity of starting materials. This means that Pruteen manufacture can continue non-stop for up to six months at a time. But what exactly *is* Pruteen? It is the dried bacterial cells.

This is used at present as an animal feed for chickens and calves. Pruteen has a relatively high *nucleic acid* content, which is harmless in animals, but can cause *gout* in some humans. If

Pruteen, packed and ready for distribution

Pruteen is well-received

51

the nucleic acids were removed so that it was safe for human consumption would you eat sausages made from bacteria? Who knows, you may soon be eating them without realizing it!

Biotechnologists at ICI had to overcome many engineering and microbiological problems in developing Pruteen.

Pruteen production has been a success in terms of growing microbes on a large scale. In terms of sales however it has not been a success. It cannot be made cheaply at present. For this reason many farmers prefer to buy animal feeds made from soya protein, as this costs less.

FARMS OR FERMENTERS?

Why is there so much interest in microbes as food? Why not develop agriculture on a bigger and better scale? It is fair to point out that microbes are very efficient protein producers, one of the reasons being that they grow rapidly. All they need are a few – often unusual – raw materials, warmth and a growth vessel. This may be a simple polythene tank or a massive steel fermenter. In either case it must not be contaminated by other microbes.

Suitable agricultural land is in short supply these days. A farm of the future may grow microbes instead of wheat or potatoes. It may consist of one or more fermentation vessels taking up relatively little land. Inside these vessels microbial food could be produced, no matter what the climate outside. The questions remain:

- Will humans eat squashed dried microbes instead of meat and vegetables?
- Will you?

SUMMARY

Traditionally, biotechnology has been used in the food industry to upgrade or preserve products. In recent years, alternative methods of food production have used microbes themselves as a source of protein-rich food.

ACTIVITY 4

Measuring the density of liquids – milk and beer

All liquids have density. This is related to the composition of the liquid.

$$\text{Density} = \frac{\text{mass of sample}}{\text{mass of an equal volume of water}}$$

Method A
You will need:

- milk
- beer
- weighing bottles
- balance

Weigh samples of milk and beer. Work out the density of each sample using the equation on the opposite page.

Does milk have the same density as beer?

Method B
You will need:

- milk
- beer
- thermometers (two)
- hydrometer cylinder
- hydrometers (1) range 1.025 to 1.035 g/cm^3
  (2) range 1.20 to 1.30 g/cm^3

The densities of milk and beer can also be measured using a **hydrometer**. You may have seen someone using a hydrometer as part of their 'home brew' programme. Different hydrometers are calibrated over different ranges. First try using a hydrometer calibrated over the range 1.025 to 1.035 g/cm^3 and one calibrated over 1.20 to 1.30 g/cm^3.

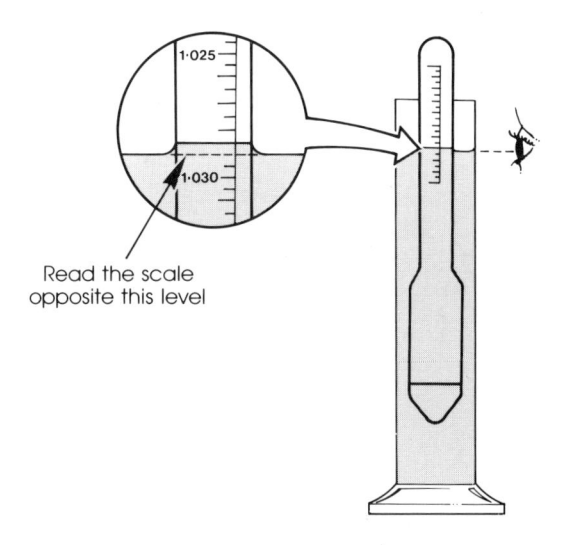

Reading the scale of a hydrometer

Read the scale opposite this level

1) (a) Allow both liquids to reach room temperature (approx 20 °C). This helps ensure that accurate readings are taken.
   (b) Pour the milk carefully into the hydrometer cylinder until it is full.

(c) Carefully lower hydrometer (1) into the milk.

(d) Allow the hydrometer to come to rest. Note the position of the meniscus on the stem. This is the density of the milk sample.
Your eye must be level with the surface of the milk when taking a reading. A small allowance should be made for the rise up the stem due to the meniscus.
The bulb of the hydrometer should not be touching the side of the cylinder.

(e) Repeat using hydrometer (2). Does this hydrometer have a suitable range to make the measurement?

2) Repeat 1) but use beer instead of milk.

3) How do your results from Method A compare with those from Method B?

4) Try three other hydrometers calibrated over different ranges. Are they suitable?

Further work

1) Compare the densities of different types of (a) milk e.g. skimmed milk, Channel Islands milk, (b) beer e.g. light ale, bitter, stout.

2) If the milk or beer is diluted with water does this affect the density?

3) Attempt to explain why density measurements are important in (a) the milk industry, (b) the beer industry.

ACTIVITY 5

Experiments with yoghurt

For a long time yoghurt making has been used as a way of preserving milk.

Carry out these investigations:

- Can all types of milk be used to make yoghurt?
- Is a starter always needed?
- What happens to the pH of the milk as it changes into yoghurt? How does this affect preservation?

Warning! You are advised not to eat or drink anything made in a science lab. If you would like to taste yoghurt made in these experiments, either work in a home economics room, or work at home, but **remember** to make sure that all containers and utensils are clean.

1) Into a yoghurt pot or beaker put some UHT milk. UHT (ultra heat treated) milk is sterilised so it does not contain microbes. Add a little natural yoghurt (starter). Mix and leave in the warmth overnight. What has happened?
2) Measure the pH of the milk (a) at the start, (b) at the end of this work. Explain any difference.
3) Repeat 1) above without using a starter. What happens?
4) Repeat 1) above, but instead of UHT milk use
   (a) ordinary pasteurised milk,
   (b) pasteurised milk which has been heated and allowed to cool,
   (c) dried milk dissolved in water.
   Can all types of milk be used to make yoghurt?

ACTIVITY 6

The action of rennin on milk

Rennet is an extract prepared from tissue in the stomach of a calf. It contains the enzyme rennin. Microbial rennin is also available nowadays.

Rennin catalyses coagulation of the milk protein called casein. As a result the milk clots to form curds. Rennet is used in the production of most cheeses.

Warning! Rennin is an enzyme and care should be taken in case of allergic reactions. Do not put the liquids near your face and wash off immediately any spilt on your skin.

Experiment 1   Effect of temperature

This experiment attempts to find answers to the following questions.

(a) How does rennin act on milk?
(b) At which temperature does rennin work best?
(c) At which temperature is rennin inactivated?

You will need:

- 3 cm^3 rennet essence
- 70 cm^3 milk
- a 1 cm^3 syringe
- a 10 cm^3 syringe
- 7 large test-tubes + rack
- waterbath, the temperature of which can be changed, **or** 6 waterbaths set at 30 °C, 35 °C, 40 °C, 50 °C, 60 °C, 70 °C
- thermometer
- stop clock

Method

(A) 1) Use a syringe (10 cm³) to place 10 cm³ of milk in each of two test-tubes.
2) Stand the tubes in a waterbath at 30 °C until the milk reaches 30 °C.
3) Do *not* add rennet essence to test-tube 1. (This is the control.)
4) Use a syringe (1 cm³) to add 0.5 cm³ of rennet essence to test-tube 2.
5) Shake test-tubes 1 and 2 immediately.
6) Start the stop clock.
7) Observe the contents of both tubes.
8) How long does it take for the milk to coagulate? (Time it in minutes.)
9) Does the milk in both test-tubes coagulate?

(B) 1) Put 10 cm³ of milk at 35 °C and 0.5 cm³ of rennet essence into a test-tube.
2) Shake the test-tube.
3) Time how long it takes for the milk to coagulate.

(C) Repeat (B) at 40 °C, 50 °C, 60 °C and 70 °C.

Tabulate your results like this.

Test-tube	Temperature (°C)	Time taken to coagulate (minutes)
1	30	
2	30	
3	35	
4	40	
5	50	
6	60	
7	70	

Show your results in a graph like this.

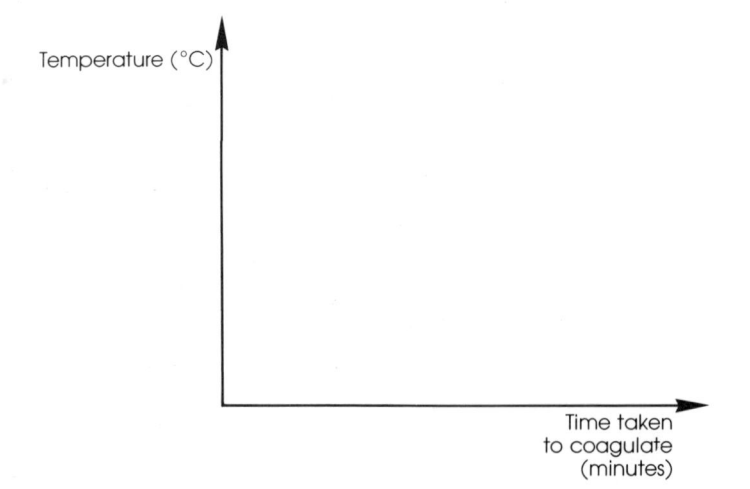

Use your results to answer the questions at the start of the experiment.

Experiment 2 Effect of pH

pH has an effect on enzyme-controlled reactions (see Chapter 2). This experiment attempts to find answers to the following questions.

(a) At which pH does rennin work best?
(b) At which pH is rennin inactivated?

You will need:

- 50 cm^3 milk
- rennet essence
- 0.1 M lactic acid solution
- 0.1 M sodium hydroxide solution
- a 10 cm^3 syringe
- 3 1 cm^3 syringes; use one for acid, one for alkali, one for rennet
- 5 large test-tubes + rack
- pH papers or pH meter
- waterbath at 35 °C
- thermometer
- stop clock

Method

1) Label the five test-tubes 1, 2, 3, 4 and 5.
   Use appropriate syringes to prepare the following:

   - test-tube 1 10 cm^3 milk + 1 cm^3 lactic acid
   - test-tube 2 10 cm^3 milk + 0.5 cm^3 lactic acid
   - test-tube 3 10 cm^3 milk only
   - test-tube 4 10 cm^3 milk + 2 cm^3 sodium hydroxide
   - test-tube 5 10 cm^3 milk + 2.5 cm^3 sodium hydroxide

2) Measure and note down the pH of each solution.

3) Place the five test-tubes in a waterbath at 35 °C and leave until the solution in each test-tube has reached 35 °C.

4) Add 0.5 cm^3 of rennet essence to each test-tube and mix.

5) Start the stop clock.

6) Note the time taken for the milk to coagulate in each test-tube.

Tabulate your results.

Show your results in a graph.

Use your results to answer questions (a) and (b) at the start of the experiment.

Experiment 3 Effect of milk heat treatment

Milk may be heat treated in different ways.

This experiment attempts to find if the type of heat treatment effects the action of rennin.

You will need:

- 10 cm^3 samples of milk of three types:
  pasteurised milk
  pasteurised milk which has been boiled and cooled
  UHT milk
- rennet essence
- a 10 cm^3 syringe
- a 1 cm^3 syringe
- 3 large test-tubes + rack
- waterbath at 35 °C
- thermometer
- stop clock

Method

1) Place 10 cm^3 of each type of milk into each of the three test-tubes.
2) Place the test-tubes in a waterbath at 35 °C and leave until each sample has reached 35 °C.
3) Add 0.5 cm^3 of rennet essence to each test-tube and mix.
4) Start the stop clock.
5) Note the time taken for the milk to coagulate in each test-tube.

Tabulate and explain your results.

Explain the significance of this activity to the cheese-making industry.

ACTIVITY 7

Fungus in cheese

Does blue cheese have fungus growing in it?

You will need:

- samples of cheese:
  Danish blue
  Bavarian blue
  Lymeswold
  Stilton
  one other type of non-blue cheese
- Bunsen burner
- inoculating loop
- 10 petri dishes containing potato dextrose agar (recipe below)
- incubator at 25 °C

Recipe for potato dextrose agar (for ten petri dishes)

Mix:
- 3.7 g dried potato
- 30 ml distilled water

Add:
- 3.3 g glucose
- 166 ml distilled water
- 2.8 g agar

Autoclave at 15 psi at 121 °C for 15 minutes.

Method

1) Sterilise the inoculating loop in a flame and allow it to cool.

2) Leave one petri dish unopened, as a control.

3) For *each* sample of blue cheese:
   (a) transfer a *small* piece of the blue vein into the agar and spread gently over the surface. Replace the lid of the petri dish immediately. Label. Sterilise the loop.
   (b) Transfer a *small* piece of the non-blue part of the cheese on to the agar and spread gently over the surface. Replace the lid of the petri dish immediately. Label. Sterilise the loop.

4) Transfer a *small* piece of the non-blue cheese on to the agar as above. Label. Sterilise the loop.

   Suggestion for labels:
   Name/class
   Date
   Type of cheese e.g. DB – Danish Blue
   Blue vein (BV) or non-blue vein (N)

5) Tape the lid of each petri dish to the base. Use four small pieces of Sellotape only.

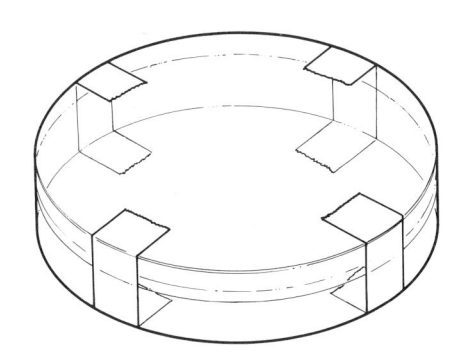

Seal the petri dish with Sellotape

6) Leave each dish in a warm place for a few days.

Tabulate your results, for example, as follows.

	Petri dish	Is fungus growing? (✓ = yes, × = no)
1	Control	
2	Cheese A. blue vein	
3	Cheese A. non blue vein	
4	etc.	
5		
6		
7		
8		
9		
10	Non-blue cheese	

Explain your results.

ACTIVITY 8

Detection of protein in microbial foods

Is protein present in all microbial foods?

You will need:

- a small amount of biuret solution
- 5 cm³ syringes:
  1 for each food sample solution
  1 for the biuret solution
- Test-tubes (1 for each sample) and rack

Obtain samples of some of these foods:

- cheese
- bread
- beer
- yoghurt
- *mycoprotein
- *Pruteen

Make a solution of each food by mixing approximately 2 g or 2 cm³ with an equal volume of water.

Method

For each sample:

1) Mix 3 cm³ of the sample with 3 cm³ of biuret solution in a test-tube.
2) Note the colour formed.

*Pruteen and mycoprotein are made by ICI at their Agricultural Division, Billingham, Cleveland.

A blue colour indicates no protein.
A violet/purple colour indicates that protein is present.

Tabulate your results.

Explain your results.

ACTIVITY 9

A mini Pruteen fermenter

Can Pruteen be made on a laboratory scale?

You will need:

- plastic drinks bottle (1.5 litre or 2 litre)
- sterilising solution e.g. Milton
- bacteria: *Methylophilus methylotrophus* (see below)*
- growth medium, 1 litre (see following page)
- aerator pump
- tubing
- air stone
- cotton wool
- waterbath at 37 °C
- inoculating loop

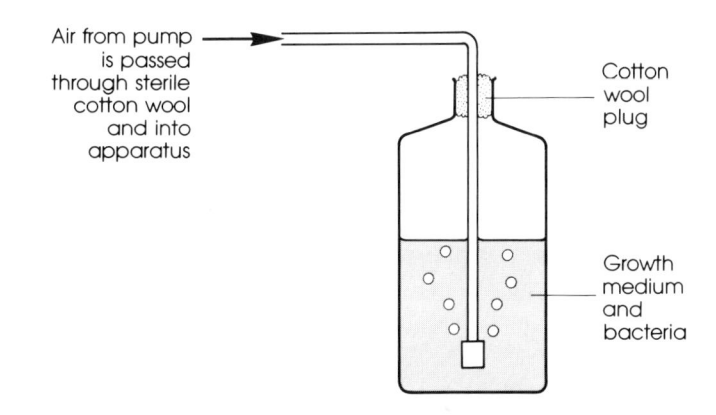

The set-up for the experiment

Air from pump is passed through sterile cotton wool and into apparatus

Cotton wool plug

Growth medium and bacteria

Method
1) Sterilise the fermenter.
2) Prepare the growth medium.
3) Transfer a few bacteria (with a sterile inoculating loop) into the growth medium.
4) Transfer the inoculated medium into the fermenter.

*Supplier of bacterial culture (*Methylophilus methylotrophus*)
NCIMB
135 Abbey Road
Aberdeen AB9 8DG

5) Place the fermenter in the waterbath at 37 °C.
6) Attach the air supply.

Note the colour of the medium each day over a seven-day period.

Problems
1) How can the apparatus be modified to show carbon dioxide production? Carbon dioxide is produced as a result of bacterial respiration. It is therefore an indication that the bacteria are alive!
2) How can dried bacterial cells (Pruteen) be obtained from the medium after seven days?
   Note Bacterial cells are very small. They would pass through filter paper.

Recipe for 1 litre of growth medium

water	960 cm^3
ammonium sulphate	1.8 g
magnesium sulphate	0.2 g
buffer: potassium hydrogen phosphate	1.9 g
sodium hydrogen phosphate (hydrated)	1.4 g
iron (III) chloride	0.001 g
solution of trace metals:	
calcium carbonate	1.8 g
1 M hydrochloric acid	36.6 cm^3
calcium sulphate (hydrated)	0.02 g
zinc sulphate (hydrated)	0.01 g
manganese sulphate	0.01 g

After sterilising by autoclaving (15 psi for 15 minutes) methanol (0.5% by volume) is added.

QUESTIONS ON CHAPTER 3

1 Give two examples of the early application of biotechnology to food production.

2 Why did people – many years ago – change milk into cheese or yoghurt?

3 What is 'food processing'? Give three examples.

4 Outline the main stages in *one* of the following.
   (a) making cheese
   (b) making bread
   (c) making beer

5 Why are some types of algae being grown as food in some hot countries?

6 Give three reasons why microbes are being grown nowadays as a source of food.

CHAPTER 4
BIOTECHNOLOGY AND FUELS

A fuel can be burnt to release energy, often in the form of heat. We burn coal, oil or natural gas to heat our homes or cook our food. These are examples of 'fossil fuels', made millions of years ago when microbes (and pressure from rock deposits) acted upon the dead remains of animals and plants. Since the 18th century, and especially in the 20th century, many of these energy or fuel reserves have been used up.

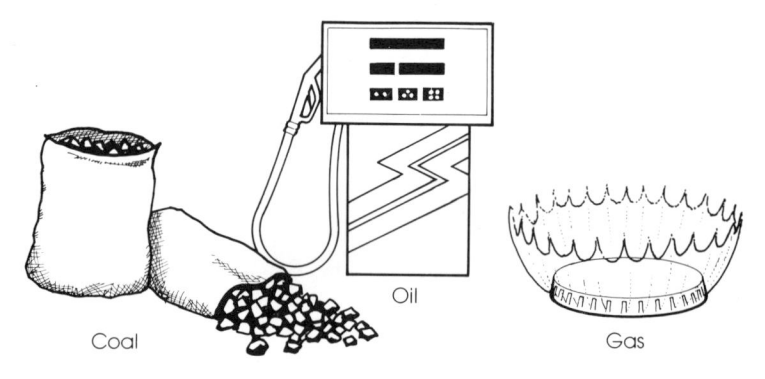

Fossil fuels

Coal   Oil   Gas

Fuels are needed to run many industrial processes. Much fuel is also used to run our cars and other types of transport.

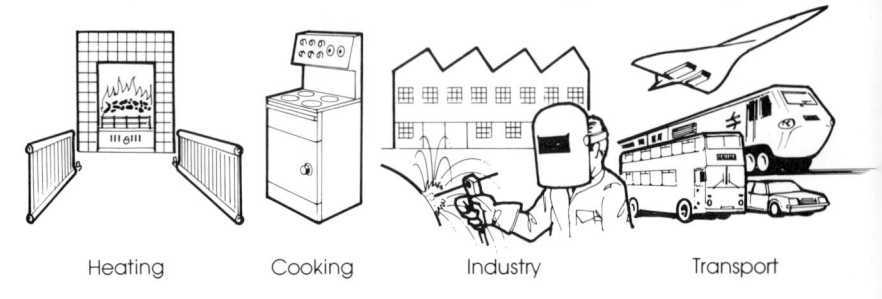

Some uses of fuels

Heating   Cooking   Industry   Transport

Can you think of any other types of fuels? Make a list in three columns as follows:

Type of fuel		
Solid	*Liquid*	*Gas*
Coal	Oil	Natural Gas

How long will it take to use up all the world's fossil fuel reserves? Some people think that they may be used up within 50 years – during your life-time.

Since the early 1970s some fuels have become expensive. Some countries do not have rich fuel reserves.

PLANTS AND ENERGY

Plants obtain their energy from sunlight. *Chlorophyll* in their leaves is used to trap the Sun's energy. This is used to convert carbon dioxide and water to carbohydrate in a process called *photosynthesis*, as we saw in Chapter 2.

Carbohydrates, such as starch or cellulose, store energy. This is released when the plant material is burned in the air.

Wood is the fuel most commonly used world-wide. In some countries it may be the only type of fuel available. The more that is used, the less there is left available. Some families in parts of Africa and India need to trek long distances each day in order to collect enough fire wood to cook a meal. Wood in renewable and can be replaced, unlike fossil fuels, but it does take a long time to grow. Wood can be burnt directly as a fuel or converted into other fuels.

BIOMASS

At present, other forms of fuel are being considered. One possible source of fuel is *biomass*. This term refers to biological raw materials, including wood, which can be changed by biotechnology into more useful and valuable fuels.

(A) Wood (fuel) $\xrightarrow{\text{burn}}$ Energy release

(B) Biomass $\xrightarrow{\text{biotechnology}}$ Fuel $\xrightarrow{\text{burn}}$ Energy release

Wood can be burnt directly or upgraded by biotechnology. Unlike wood, fuel produced in (B) can be burnt in an internal combustion engine.

Biomass is simply any material which is derived from photosynthesis.

Biomass can be subdivided into three main groups. These are *energy crops, natural vegetation* and *wastes*. Our conventional sources of energy – coal, gas and oil – all started as biomass.

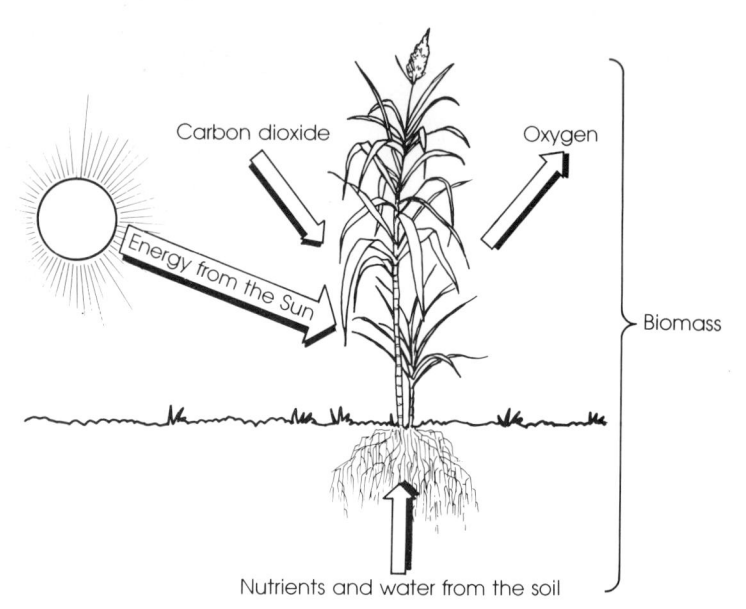

Producing biomass

Unlike fossil fuels, however, biomass is *renewable*. Some types of biomass, such as wastes, are readily available, cheap and plentiful in the long term. Usually, biomass is converted into *ethanol* (a liquid) or *methane* (a gas). Both are high-grade fuels.

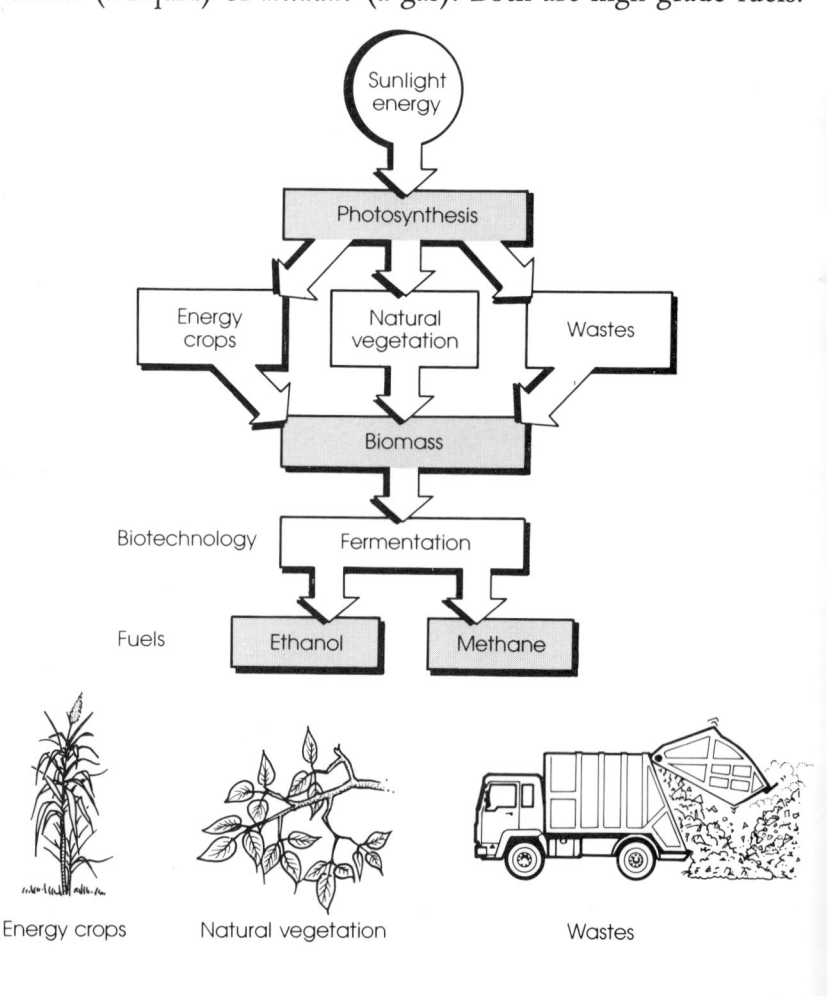

Photosynthesis, biomass and fuels

Types and sources of biomass

Biomass

ETHANOL FROM BIOMASS

There are other uses of alcohol besides in drinks such as beer or wine! The major bulk chemical produced by biotechnology is ethanol, an alcohol. It is made, under certain conditions, when microbial cells, such as yeasts, react with plant material.

All cells, including microbes, are efficient *energy converters*. They need an energy supply (food) for *respiration*, to release energy for life-processes such as *moving* and *growing*. Yeast cells can use sugars as a source of food. When oxygen is available the yeast converts the sugars into energy, with carbon dioxide and water as waste products. Relatively large amounts of energy are released.

However if oxygen is not available the yeast can still respire, although less energy is released. Some of this energy is stored as alcohol. Brewers have taken advantage of yeast's ability to respire without oxygen, a process sometimes called *fermentation*, for centuries. As far as yeast is concerned alcohol, like carbon dioxide and water which are also produced, is a waste product. The alcohol accumulates because there is not enough oxygen available. Not only is this alcohol a waste product it is also harmful to the yeast. If its concentration reaches a certain level the yeast is killed. No fun for the yeast!

How to keep yeast cells happy

No oxygen
Little alcohol

No oxygen
Too much alcohol

67

But what has this to do with fuels? In the 1970s and 1980s some countries, Brazil in particular, started to grow sugar cane plants on very large areas of land to be used as fuel. Food or fuel? Think about it! Traditionally, land was used to grow crops as food. Now land is being used in some countries to grow fuels. Will people in these countries have enough food?

CASE STUDY 9

Sugar to fuel

The Brazilian government made a decision to grow sugar cane on a large scale as a source of fuel and by the mid-1980s about a billion litres of ethanol per year were being produced from it. But why?

Sugar cane is grown

The sugar cane is transported to a nearby fermentation plant

Brazil does not have fossil fuel reserves, nor can it afford to buy in expensive oil. But it does have large areas of land available, as well as a warm climate suitable for growing crops quickly.

Other countries, including Zambia and Zimbabwe, have made a similar decision. In the USA maize, not sugar, is grown as a fuel source.

In this plant, the sugar cane is crushed to separate the sugar juice from the stalks; the stalks are burnt, as a source of energy in the fermentation plant

Yeast is mixed with the sugar juice inside a fermenter

The end product of fermentation is distilled, to produce ethanol

Instead of filling their tanks with petrol, drivers in Brazil are using ethanol, derived from sugar cane, as fuel. There is an incentive, because fuel alcohol is on sale at about half the price of petrol. It costs about £250 to convert an ordinary petrol engine so that it can burn ethanol efficiently. Some engines can be powered without conversion by using a mixture of petrol and ethanol called *gasohol*. The Brazilian government decided to use gasohol instead of pure ethanol to

69

stop people from drinking the fuel on sale: 'Let's have a party down at the fuel station! Five litres of alcohol and ten glasses!'

Ethanol is transported away to be used

Cars use alcohol as fuel

Can biotechnology meet the challenge?

What challenges lie ahead for the biotechnologists in the fuel industry? The crucial factor with any product of biotechnology is that it must compete in the market place with similar products made by other processes. Alcohol from biomass will only sell if it is cheap and can compete successfully with alcohol produced by the chemical industries, as well as traditional fuels such as petrol.

What can biotechnologists do to cut costs, improve efficiency and produce cheap products? With alcohol fuel some possibilities include:

1 Develop strains of yeast which can tolerate high levels of ethanol
Most yeast cells die if the concentration of ethanol reaches 12–15%. New strains of top fermenting yeasts have been developed which withstand very much higher alcohol levels. In present-day fuel alcohol factories it is expensive to purify

alcohol from the mixture of materials in the fermentation vessel. Normally this mixture is boiled and the vapour is cooled to give fairly pure ethanol. This process requires heat, which is expensive to provide. If strains of yeast could be developed to withstand higher levels of alcohol – say 30% – the distillation costs would be cut. Someone, somewhere will be working on this problem at present no doubt!

2 Use plants other than sugar cane as a raw material

Sugar cane plants grow quickly in warm climates and efficiently convert sunlight energy into sugar. The sugar cane juice is fermented on a large scale into fuel alcohol. But sugar as a crop also has a high value as food. Why not sell sugar as food and grow less valuable crops for fuels? A wide range of plants are receiving close attention. One such crop is *cassava*, a root crop which grows throughout the tropics on poor soils. It does not however contain as much sugar as sugar cane, but can enzymes be used to change stored food into sugars? Will microbes other than yeasts be used to break down the stored foods into sugars? Can strains of yeast be developed which can feed directly on the stored foods? These are possibilities and are just some of the problems which biotechnologists are attempting to solve in the fuel crisis story. The chances are, however, that by the time *you* are driving your own car you will be asking for 4-star alcohol at your local filling-station!

METHANE FROM BIOMASS

Gas from waste

Traditional methods of agriculture produce animal waste in fairly small quantities. These can easily be returned to the land as fertiliser. Modern intensive methods of rearing animals, however, produce large amounts of waste. These cannot easily be disposed of on land. They are also troublesome to handle and store. The farmers have an additional responsibility. They must take care not to pollute nearby streams and rivers as this in turn could affect water supplies.

The farmers have a problem. They want maximum use of the waste as fertiliser. They must also avoid pollution with the large quantities of waste which are produced.

One solution to this problem is to produce *biogas* from waste. Fermentation of the waste, in the absence of air, produces biogas. This consists of about 60% methane with carbon dioxide and other gases. The solid material left after this process is a good fertiliser.

Methane production is a natural process. It occurs whenever dead plant or animal material rots where no air is available. This occurs in muds of *marshes* and in the stomachs of *herbivores* such as cows. Is a cow a living, mobile fermenter?

Methane is the major component of natural gas such as that extracted from beneath the North Sea. In this case many types of microbes, over a long time period, have decomposed organic matter into methane gas. The large reserves of this gas are now being tapped as a fuel.

Biogas – the benefits

On farms, manure and other wastes are allowed to decompose in closed tanks from which air has been excluded. The biogas produced is used as a fuel on the farm and to produce electricity. Some of this fuel is needed to keep the tank warm, as biogas production occurs most efficiently at about 35 °C. The solid material left is used as a fertiliser.

Biogas production

CASE STUDY 10

DIY fuel on the farm

In Kent, a farmer milks his cows using electric power from the waste produced by those cows. The waste is drained away into a nearby tank. The manure is decomposed by bacteria. The methane produced is used to drive an electric generator which previously ran on diesel oil. Power from muck! Waste not, want not! This example is typical of many farms in the UK today.

SIMPLE BIOGAS DIGESTERS

There are vast numbers of these biogas digesters in use throughout the world, especially in China and India. Here they provide cheap fuel used for heating, cooking and lighting in the home. A family usually has an area to store wastes, such as a hole in the ground or a closed tank. All domestic and animal wastes are fed into it.

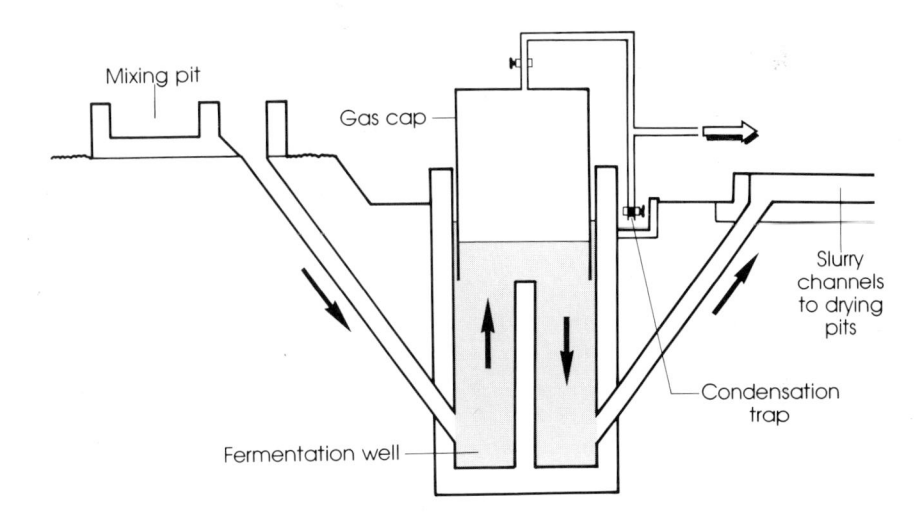

A biogas plant, of Indian design

A typical family of six keeps about six animals. The animal, human and household waste is collected daily and placed into a biogas fermenter. As a result, enough gas is produced to supply the fuel needed by the family each day.

This type of biotechnology is most suitable for *small-scale* operations. This is because the raw materials are collected *locally*. The resulting fuel is also used *locally*, so there are no extra costs, such as transport.

The process of *decomposition* is complex and slow. It has two main stages. The *first* is the *acid-forming* stage. Acid-forming bacteria break down the waste products into simple organic acids. Water must be present. The acid-formers themselves are found living naturally in animal and human waste. The *second stage* involves methane-forming bacteria. These act on the organic acids produced in the first stage, and gas is produced.

Digested sludge, left as solid waste, can be used as fertiliser. It is interesting to note therefore that biogas production involves *mixed* populations of bacteria. Other fermentation processes, such as Pruteen production, involve only *one* type of bacterium. Also, the methane-producing bacteria work only in the absence of air.

This tractor in China runs on a mixture of biogas and diesel oil

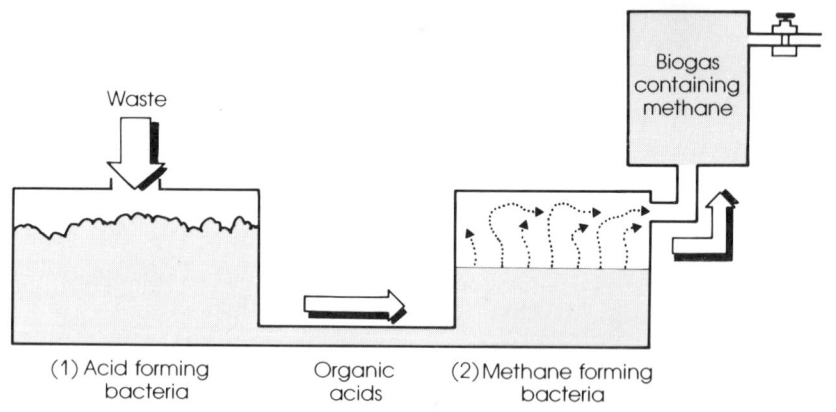

Production of biogas

Waste

Biogas containing methane

(1) Acid forming bacteria   Organic acids   (2) Methane forming bacteria

Note (A) (1) and (2) consist of mixed populations of bacteria, not just one type of bacterium.

(B) (2) work only in the absense of air.

CASE STUDY 11

Biogas from landfill sites

Rubbish is a source of energy. Rubbish tips nowadays are usually *landfill sites*. They are large holes in the ground, into which rubbish has been tipped. Some older, (perhaps 20 years old) large sites are now being used as sources of *biogas*. This gas is formed by the action of microbes, in the absence of oxygen, on the rubbish. Over a period of time, biogas collects in the tip.

Biogas from a waste tip is used at Birkenhead

Pipes are installed to draw off the biogas which has been generated. This can then be used as an *energy source* to provide heat or generate electricity.

One such source has been developed in Bedfordshire. A brick company's disused clay pit has been used as a landfill site. Biogas from the rubbish is piped to the brickworks and used to heat nearby kilns.

In some cases there has been co-operation between council rubbish tips and local companies. A joint venture between Merseyside County Council and Cadbury-Schweppes started in 1985. Biogas from a very large landfill site in Birkenhead is piped to the nearby factory where sweets and biscuits are made. The biogas is used to generate electricity for use in the factory.

If water is pumped into landfill sites, biogas production may be increased. Even a small *gas pit* can produce enough fuel to operate a small turbine for the generation of electricity. This has possibilities for small, self-contained communities.

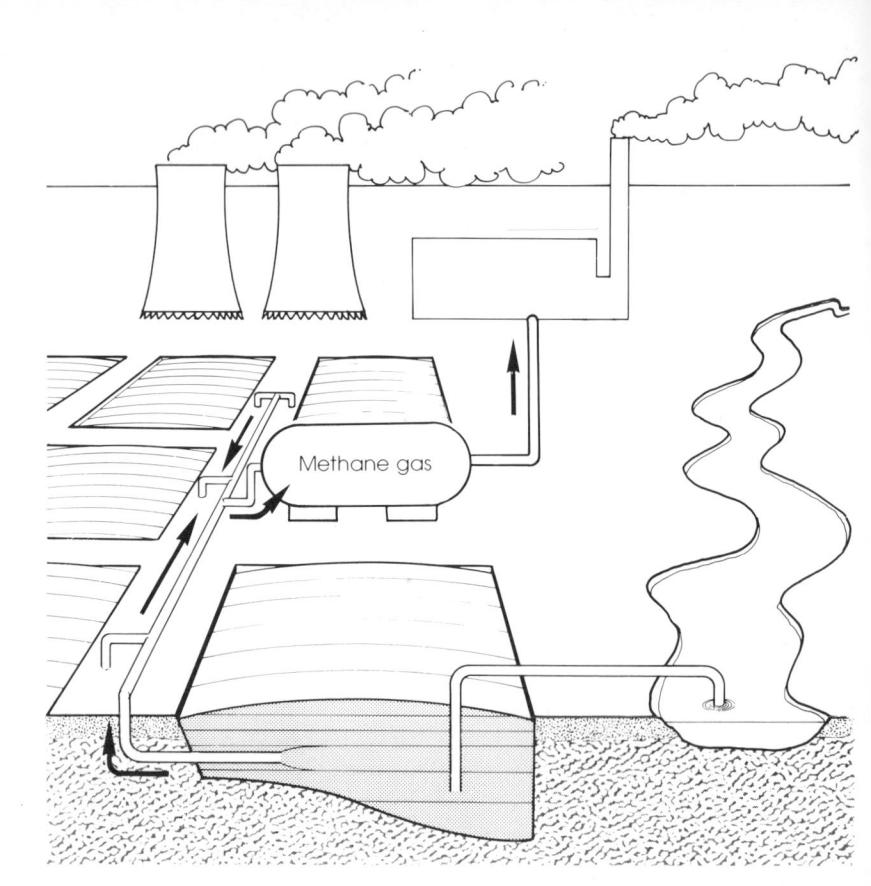

Biogas from landfill waste

The biogas pumping station at Bidston tip

BIOMASS, BIOTECHNOLOGY, WHAT ELSE?

CASE STUDY 12

Put an oil-palm in your tank!

Some plants produce natural oils. These need little processing and engines can run on them. The day of home-grown fuel for transport may not be far off!

Vegetable oils are produced by plants such as oil-palms, sunflowers, peanuts, olives and maize. Concern about health has encouraged the use of vegetable oils, rather than animal fats. It may not be long however before these oils are being generally used as fuels for transport. At present they do work in some engines, but are too expensive.

Oil-palm-powered transport

They can be used pure, or blended with other fuels such as diesel or alcohol. Plant oil is therefore a promising alternative to alcohol when it comes to turning biomass into fuels. Vegetable oils have the advantage, in that it is easier to extract the fuel. No fermentation is required. The oil is just squeezed out of the plants!

In 1980 Brazil began to look at alternatives to sugar cane as a source of fuel. They are at present investigating a wide range of biomass material for fuel production. In one trial, buses in the capital city of Brasilia were run on a mixture of 73% diesel oil, 20% palm oil and 7% ethanol. The results were promising and palm oil is being seriously considered as an *extender* to be mixed with existing fuels.

There are some other advantages in making fuel from palm oil, rather than making ethanol from sugar. As well as it being easier to extract the fuel from the palms, year-round production is possible by continuous harvesting. The by-products are less of a pollution problem. Also one of the *by-products* of the process is a protein-rich animal food. Water is not needed during the processing of the fuel and the whole plant can be used to make a number of products (see p. 7). Will oil-palms in places like Malaysia and Brazil be the source of tomorrow's fuel?

Oil-palms:
the diesel fuel of
tomorrow?

CASE STUDY 13

More oil from oil wells

Alcohol from sugar is one example of an alternative fuel. It may be used instead of traditional fuels such as oil. However, biotechnology can also help fuel production *directly in the oil industry* by making it possible to obtain more oil from existing reserves.

Oil is found in underground *reservoirs*. It does not exist as large lakes however, but rather as spaces within rocks. These rocks are like sponges or honeycombs containing pores full of a mixture of oil and water. The oil is recovered by drilling into the rock and draining it from the rock pores into an oil well.

When oil is first drilled existing pressures cause it to gush to the surface. As more oil is taken the pressure drops until it is too low to drive oil from the rock pores up to the surface. These first stages of oil recovery are called *primary production*.

More oil can be obtained by increasing the pressure in the underground reservoir, a stage called *secondary production*. This can be done by injecting water or gas into the rock containing oil. However, this soon becomes too expensive, because the amount of oil produced eventually falls. This means that the money spent on pumping out a small amount of oil cannot be justified.

At this stage about two-thirds of the existing oil reserves *are still below the ground*. The oil is still in the rock at the end of secondary recovery because it sticks to the rock. Attempts to move these large quantities of oil remaining in the world's oil fields are called *tertiary* or *enhanced recovery* methods. This is where biotechnology becomes important.

Materials such as *xanthan gum* can be mixed with water and pumped into wells to make more recovery of oil possible. This gum is made by a type of bacterium called *Xanthomonas*. It acts as a *detergent* to help 'push' more oil from the rock pores underground. At present the bacteria producing the gum are grown in factories, the gum is extracted and then pumped into oil fields.

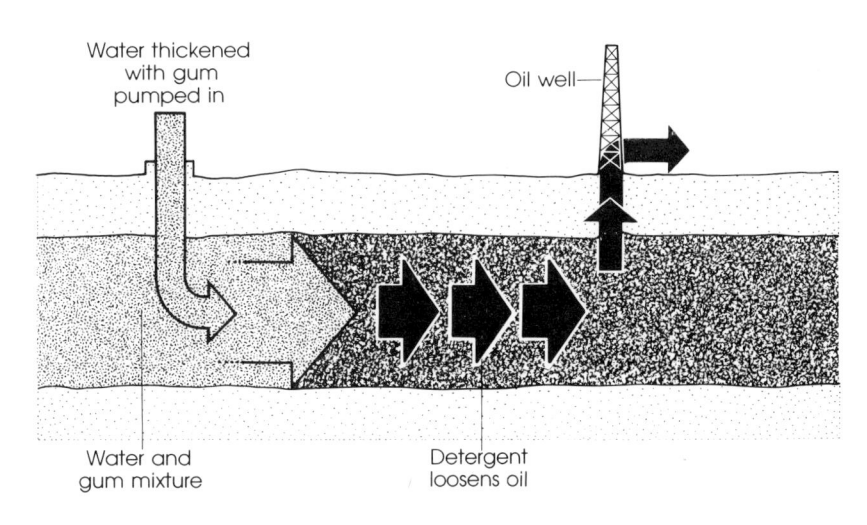

Using xanthan gum to recover oil

Some oil companies are, however, sending the bacteria themselves underground instead. Nutrients are fed to the bacteria while they are deep below the ground. The bacteria grow, produce the chemicals that help wash the oil free and produce gases which help force the oil to the surface. They are able to do this even though conditions of high temperature and pressure exist deep underground. This type of work is still being developed, but has vast potential for making much more fuel oil available from existing underground reserves.

CASE STUDY 14

Beyond biomass

At present many countries are considering biomass as a source of renewable fuel. As a result of photosynthesis biomass is produced. This is converted to fuel. The ultimate goal of scientists working on biomass is to produce energy directly from photosynthesis.

One possibility would be to split water – which does happen in photosynthesis – *directly* into oxygen and hydrogen. This hydrogen could then be used as an efficient, non-polluting, renewable fuel.

At present the hydrogen from photosynthesis is used by plants to make their own plant material. In future can photosynthesis be used directly to release hydrogen as a fuel? It's a possibility! Who knows?

Beyond biomass – hydrogen from photosynthesis without plants?

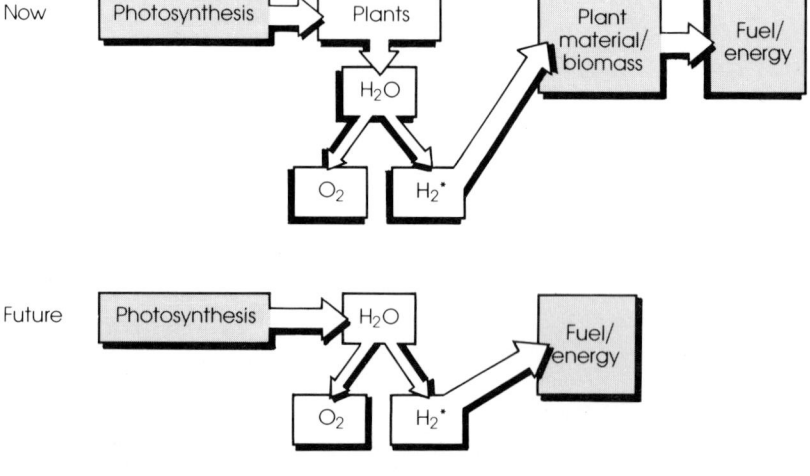

Now: Photosynthesis → Plants → H_2O → O_2, H_2* → Plant material/biomass → Fuel/energy

Future: Photosynthesis → H_2O → O_2, H_2* → Fuel/energy

*This hydrogen is bound to a chemical and is not a gas

SUMMARY

Traditional fuels will eventually be used up. Biotechnology can be used either to make more of these fuels (e.g. oil) available or as a means of making alternative types of fuel. Plant or waste material may be converted by microbes into fuels which are renewable.

ACTIVITY 10

Gas from waste

Make your own biogas digester. Here is a suggestion.

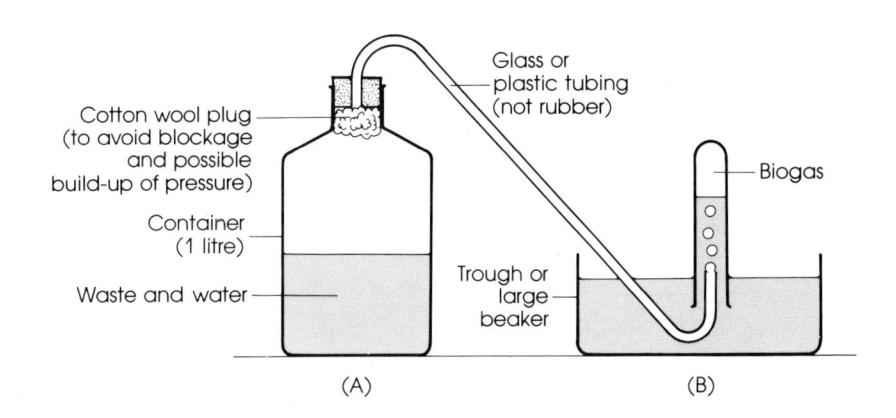

The set-up for the experiment

Tips
- Try to keep the temperature at about 30 °C.
- Wear plastic disposable gloves when handling wastes.
- Use a cotton wool plug (see diagram)
- Try to make sure that all fittings are tight.
- The fermenter should be no more than half full.
- **Always** take advice from your teacher. Gases can explode. **Do not** try this experiment at home!
- You may prefer to use sugar beet pulp instead of waste material.

Questions

1) Does the type of waste used affect the amount of gas produced? Try cow, horse, chicken manure. Mix with an equal volume of water. Is gas produced if compost is used? Does a manure/compost mixture produce gas?

2) Can different types of fermenters be used e.g. drinks bottle, glass conical flask, round-bottomed flask?

3) For how long is the biogas fermenter active?
4) What happens if the temperature (a) rises? (b) falls?
5) What is the best method of collecting gas?
6) Can the volume of gas produced be measured?
7) Is *any* biogas produced during the first (a) seven days? (b) ten days?

Here is a suggestion for modifying the set-up above, to answer questions 5) and 6).

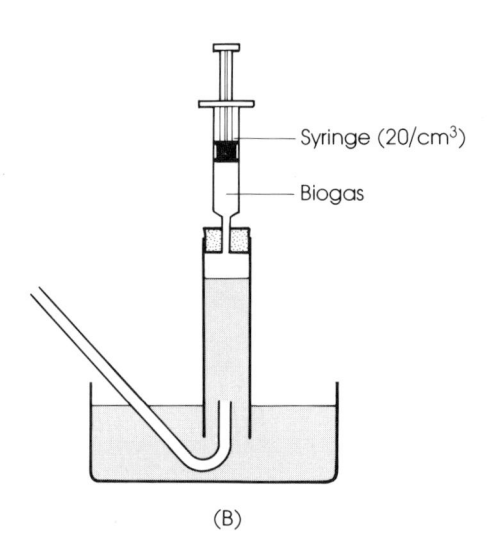

A suggestion for a modification

Syringe (20/cm^3)
Biogas

(B)

Does the gas in the syringe burn?

ACTIVITY 11

Home-made fuel?

Rather than relying on buying fuels, assume that your household would wish to be self-sufficient.

Which type of fuel would you attempt to produce? Why?

How? Design a fermenter and/or small-scale industrial process for this purpose.

What raw material would you use? Why?

Warning Do **not** try to use this fermenter before asking for expert advice. Some fuels can cause explosions!

QUESTIONS ON CHAPTER 4

1 (a) Briefly explain what is meant by
  (i) a non-renewable fuel, (ii) a renewable fuel.
  (b) Give two examples of each.

2 What is biomass?

3 (a) Explain the difference between respiration *with* oxygen and respiration *without* oxygen in terms of
  (i) energy production, (ii) alcohol production.
  (b) Name one organism that can respire with or without oxygen.

4 Why did the Brazilian Government decide to produce fuel alcohol from sugar on a large scale?

5 One of the major problems – in terms of economics and efficiency – in alcohol production from sugar is that much energy is needed to heat the fermented sugar juice and distil it into alcohol. How do you think the Brazilians have solved this energy problem?
Hint They have only used materials already available and have *not* used coal, oil or natural gas, which would be expensive to buy.

6 What is gasohol?

7 (a) In general terms, why do biotechnologists attempt to cut costs and improve efficiency?
  (b) Give one example of how they are trying to do this in fuel alcohol production.

8 (a) When drilling for oil explain what is meant by the following terms, making the differences clear.
  (i) primary recovery
  (ii) secondary recovery
  (iii) tertiary or enhanced recovery
  (b) At what stage does biotechnology become important?
  (c) How is biotechnology being used in an attempt to obtain more oil from oil wells?

9 In terms of 'using microbes' mention one basic difference between foods such as Pruteen production compared with methane production.

10 What is biogas?

WORDFINDER ON BIOTECHNOLOGY AND FUELS

Copy the grid below (or photocopy this page – teachers please see note at the front of the book) and then find the answers to the clues. One has been ringed. There are 19 more words to find. The words read from right to left or left to right horizontally, from top to bottom or bottom to top vertically, or diagonally. You can use the same letter more than once. Do not write on this page.

N	O	I	T	A	L	L	I	T	S	I	D
O	R	M	L	X	E	T	P	S	O	K	U
I	E	R	A	G	U	S	A	A	L	X	R
T	S	P	O	N	F	M	J	E	I	A	L
C	E	O	C	V	O	E	M	Y	Z	N	E
U	R	S	I	I	W	L	A	K	A	T	N
D	V	U	B	L	O	H	V	N	R	H	A
O	O	L	O	H	O	S	A	G	B	A	H
R	I	T	O	E	D	J	S	C	E	N	T
P	R	C	B	A	K	H	S	M	U	G	E
Z	L	P	J	T	C	P	A	R	A	U	M
A	Y	G	R	E	N	E	C	S	E	M	T

1. Common source of fuel which is replaceable (4)
2. Used for drinking or for running a car in some parts of the world (7)
3. We need this at home for cooking etc. (4)
4. Material which will release energy when it is burnt (4)
5. Substance which converts sugar to energy used in brewing, baking and alcohol production (5)
6. Process used to purify alcohol (12)
7. Mixture of petrol and ethanol (7)
8. Root crop (7)
9. Example of a fossil fuel (4)
10. Oil is found in one of these (9)
11. Forestry wastes, bracken and algae are examples of sources of this (7)
12. Material used to 'push' oil out of underground rock (7,3)
13. In the oil industry, primary, secondary and tertiary are the three stages of ___ (10)
14. Another type of energy crop, grown as cane (5)
15. Component of biogas (7)
16. Sunflower and olive are two types (3)
17. Example of a country which grows sugar cane as a source of fuel (6)
18. Methane is one (3)
19. Fuel is used to produce ___ (6)
20. Biological catalyst – it controls chemical reactions within a cell (6)

CHAPTER 5
BIOTECHNOLOGY AND WATER

Most of the industries that are based on biotechnology deal with water treatment and purification. We need pure water to remain healthy and to use in industrial processes. We also need to get rid of human waste and factory wastes. In the UK each person uses large volumes of pure water daily and produces about 180 litres of sewage or waste water. However, recent figures show that only 25% of the population in all developing countries have access to supplies of safe water and the use of adequate *sanitation*. The water industry in the UK has developed since the mid-nineteenth century.

DRINKING WATER

Drinking water is a valuable product. It is made fit for humans to drink by passing it through a *water purification plant*.

Rainwater is collected and stored in *reservoirs*, where exposure to sunlight and air helps to kill some of the harmful microbes. It then passes slowly through *filter beds*. These are large areas containing gravel and fine sand. Microbes grow in a 'layer' on the gravel and sand particles and form a *filtering material*. This separates out all the unwanted impurities, including those microbes which cause dangerous diseases such as *typhoid* and *cholera*. Small quantities of *chlorine* are also added to the water. This will kill any remaining microbes. Before the water is distributed to our taps it is tested for purity. These processes are shown on p. 86.

WASTE WATER

Waste water has been a problem since humans started to live together in villages and towns. Only during the last 100 years or so have adequate measures been taken to deal with it. Before that, waste water was thrown into *open sewers* in the streets or poured directly into rivers or seas. This caused *pollution problems* and resulted in outbreaks of disease.

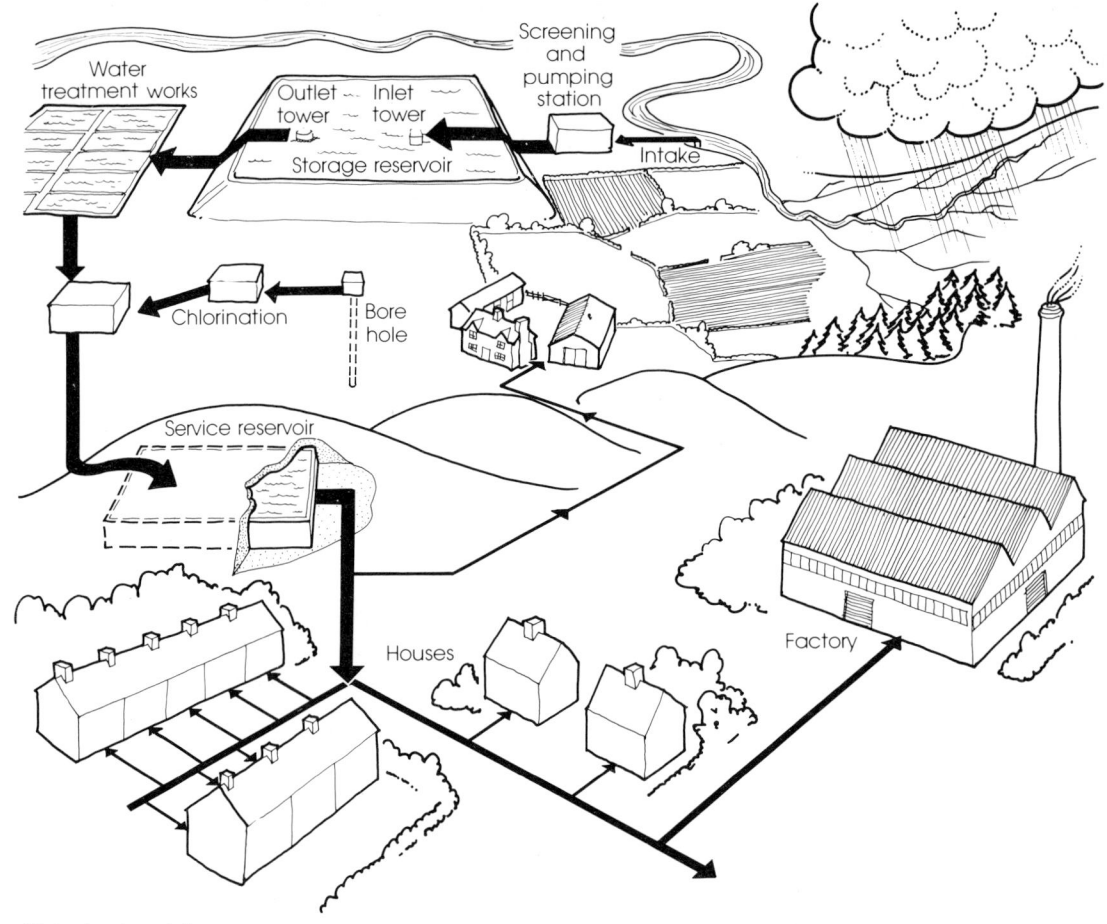

Water treatment: how our water is prepared for us (see p. 85)

There are different types of waste water. That from baths, showers and sinks or rainwater from roads and pavements is fairly harmless. Water used for cooling at power stations or steelworks is again quite clean and can be pumped directly into a river or re-used without further treatment.

Our bodies' waste products – *urine* and *faeces* – are carried away by water to form a liquid called *sewage*. This, together with most industrial waste water, is a potential pollution problem and must be treated before being re-used.

Septic tanks

Isolated houses not on main drainage often have *septic tanks* to deal with sewage treatment on a small scale. The septic tank, which is buried in the ground, consists of a large sealed tank with two pipes. One of the pipes allows sewage to enter, the other allows treated water to flow away.

As the sewage enters the tank, solids settle to the bottom. Naturally occurring microbes, which grow on a bed of coke or brick, break down the sewage. *Methane gas* is given off as a by-product. The treated water is allowed to escape into the surrounding soil or is poured into a nearby river. Solid *sludge*, which settles out is collected periodically.

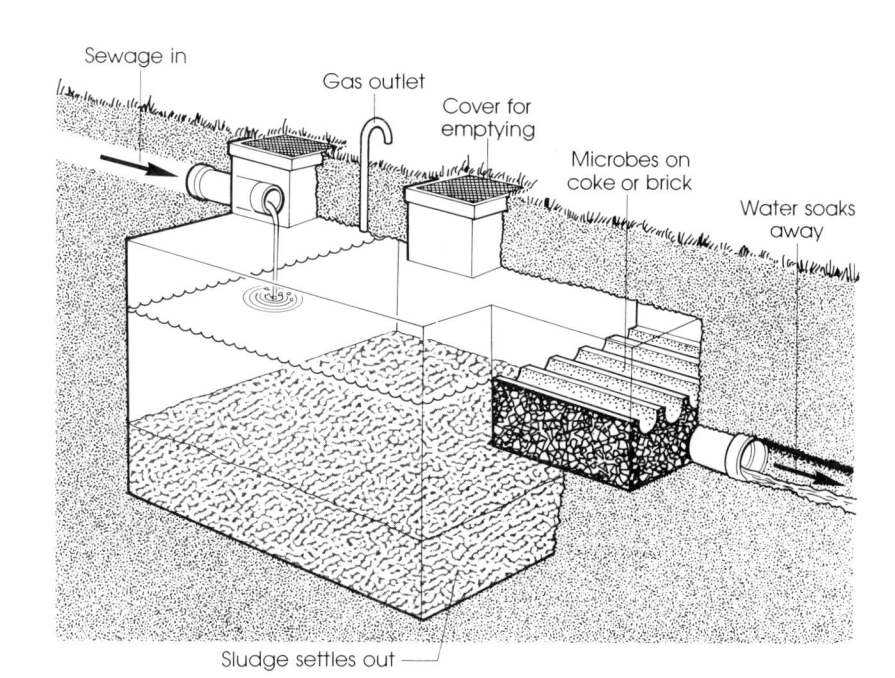

Septic tanks are still in use, for treating sewage; the sludge has to be cleaned out occasionally

Large-scale waste water treatment

The overall aim of waste water treatment is the *removal and breakdown of material*. In most other biotechnological processes it is the *production of material* which is important.

A mixed population of microbes, acting as *scavengers*, use waste substances in the water as a source of food. The waste waters and microbes are brought into contact long enough for the organisms to break down and remove *pollutants*. Complex compounds in the sewage are broken down into simple end products such as carbon dioxide or methane, which are given off as a gas. Water is purified and solids (*sludge*) are left.

The gases can be used as fuel. The purified water may then be poured into a river or given further treatment at a water-purification plant before being re-used as drinking water. The solids may be suitable for fertilisers or soil conditioner.

There are several well-established methods for treating sewage. Suspended solids and organic matter are separated from the sewage before it is poured into a river or the sea. A typical *sewage treatment works* uses processes in the following order:

1 Screens
These are metal bars spaced closely together. They remove large solids. These are burnt or buried.

2 Grit-removal channels
Grit and sand from roads and gardens is carried along in the sewage. This is removed by letting the sewage flow slowly through channels. The grit drops to the bottom and then it is disposed of by burying.

3 Primary sedimentation tanks
In these tanks the heavier organic solids settle out to be recovered as *primary sludge*, which is then pumped to the *sludge digestion plant*.

4 Biological treatment
Oxygen is necessary for this process which is sometimes called *aerobic biological treatment* or *aeration*. In these tanks the remaining organic matter in the sewage is, in part, oxidised to carbon dioxide and water. The remainder is converted by microbes to *secondary sludge*.

There are two commonly used aerobic biological treatments:

- **Biological filters or trickling filter systems** Here the waste water is sprayed through rotating arms on to a bed of crushed stones or coke, which is about two metres thick. A mixed population of microbes becomes established on the stones. As sewage trickles downwards air is forced upwards through the filter. Fungi, bacteria, protozoa and algae work together to break down the sewage.

- **Activated sludge system** Here large volumes of air are compressed and forced through sewage in a tank. After a time suspended particles join together into tiny jelly-like masses called *activated sludge*. This is swarming with microbes which thrive on the organic matter. They break it down speedily and efficiently, so that after about eight hours most of the impurities are destroyed.

5 Final settlement tanks
In these tanks biological solids settle out and are recovered as more secondary sludge. The liquid from the tanks is poured into the river or sea.

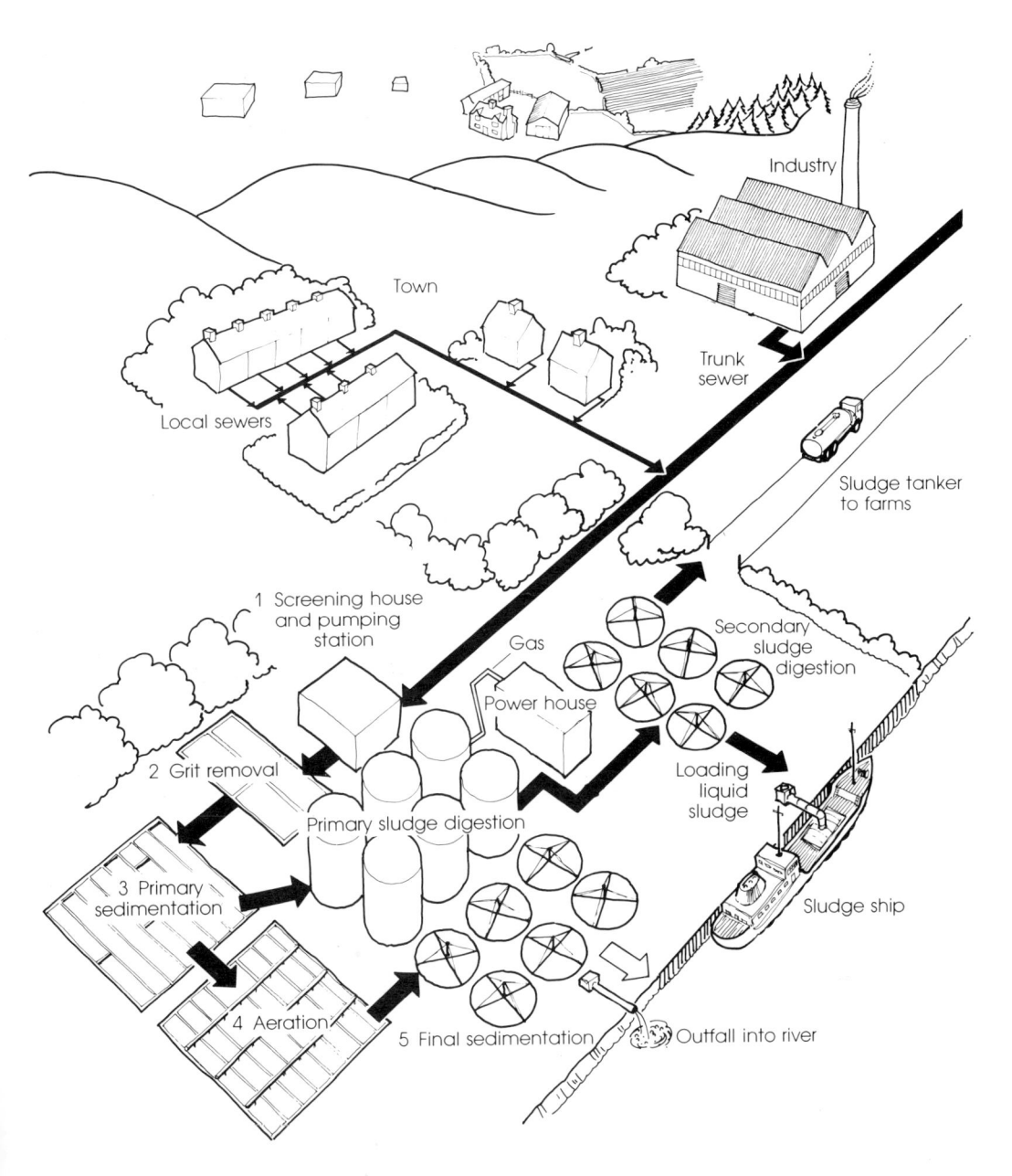

Sewage treatment: how our waste is dealt with

6 Sludge handling and disposal

Typically the primary and secondary sludges are mixed. They are then stabilised in *anaerobic digestion tanks* before disposal. Anaerobic respiration occurs in the absence of oxygen. In these tanks the organic matter is converted into methane gas and carbon dioxide. This process takes about four weeks. The gas produced is used as a fuel within the sewage works. The remaining *digested* sludge is disposed of on land or in the sea.

CASE STUDY 15

The deep shaft process

One of the problems with existing sewage farms is that large areas of land are needed for the various treatment tanks. A deep shaft process has recently been developed. It is like an *inverted fermenter* buried underground. It allows sewage treatment to take place below ground level and uses up less land than the activated sludge process.

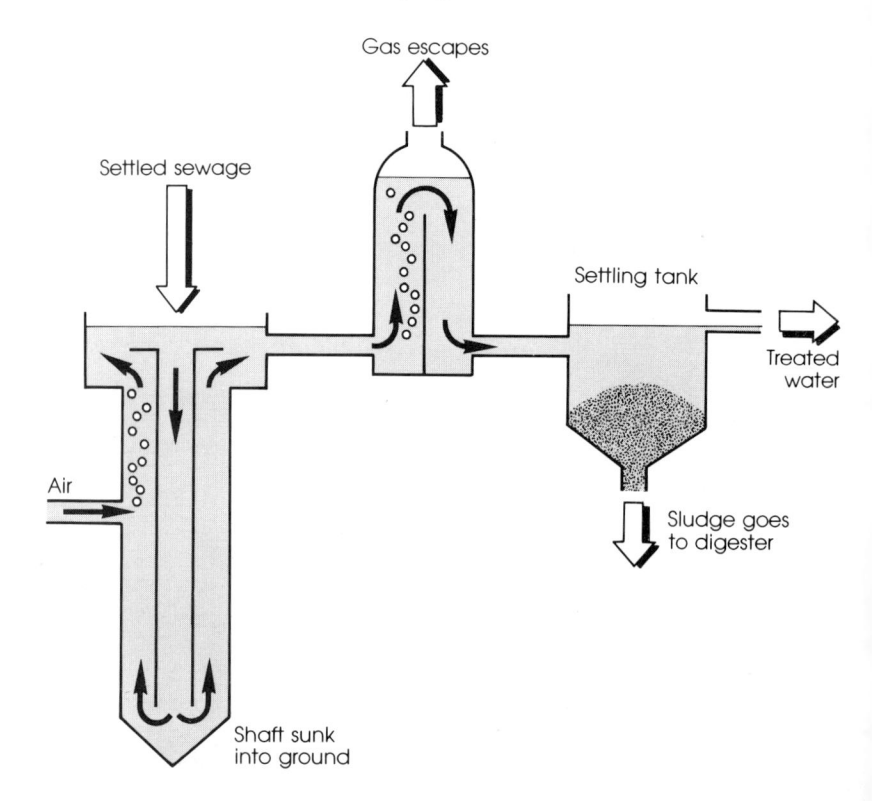

The deep shaft process for treatment of waste

CLEAN WATER: SOME PROBLEMS

Rivers are often used as a source of water to be purified before drinking or to receive water which has been treated in sewage treatment works. In recent years there has been a campaign for cleaner rivers in Britain.

New products often have undesirable side-effects. This was the case with *synthetic detergents*. Soap was used for washing people and their clothes until the late 1940s. At that time detergents were developed and widely used in industry and to clean clothes. These detergents contained some chemicals which could not be readily broken down (*degraded*) by biological action. The result was – for some years – unsightly detergent foam floating on our rivers. Nowadays most detergents are *biodegradable* (can be broken down by natural means).

Detergent foam used to be seen on rivers in the 1950s

In recent years new pollution problems have been caused by the widespread use of toxic pesticides and metals. We now realise that improper disposal of wastes of any kind can be anti-social and short-sighted. Laws have been passed to help with pollution control. Also, education has raised public awareness of the importance of pollution control. Nowadays industry is not allowed to pour poisonous wastes directly into our sewage systems and rivers. As a result many of our industrial rivers, which had been without fish for about 30 years, now have a variety of fish, including salmon.

Some of our rivers are now clean enough for fish to live in them again

SUMMARY

Drinking water is purified and waste water is treated in works which rely heavily on the action of mixed populations of microbes. Harmful materials are broken down, thereby offering a valuable and necessary service to our community. In terms of volume, the water industry is the largest of any biotechnology industries.

ACTIVITY 12

How much water do you use?

Keep a record of how much water you **use** daily. Include everything! You may be surprised at the answer.

How does your answer compare with
(a) other members of your family?
(b) other members of your class?

ACTIVITY 13

What we know about water

Carry out a survey of a number of people in your area. You may like to devise a questionnaire for this purpose. Try to investigate their knowledge of the water industry.

You may ask them:

- What do they know of water treatment?
- Do they know the difference between water purification and waste-water treatment?
- How much water do they use daily?
- How much sewage do they produce daily? (Our bodies' wastes are diluted by water each time we flush the toilet. How much?)
- How important is clean water for healthy living?
- Which diseases are carried in dirty water?
- How are present-day water pollution problems being avoided?

Which other questions should you include?

ACTIVITY 14

Visit a water treatment centre

Contact either your local water purification plant or local sewage works. Obtain permission for a visit. (You could ask for help from your teacher or an adult so that a group of you could go together.) Ask if you can take slides/photographs of the main stages of treatment at the works. Ask permission to interview one of the workers. Take a tape-cassette recorder and record the conversation, which may be about (a) a typical day's work or (b) the main stages of treatment at the works.

Compare your slides/photographs or tape with those of your friends.

QUESTIONS ON CHAPTER 5

1 Outline the main stages in the purification of drinking water.

2 What is sewage?

3 What are septic tanks and how do they work?

4 Give one basic difference between waste water treatment and most other biotechnological processes.

5 (a) In simple terms briefly summarise how microbes carry out large scale waste water treatment.
   (b) What are the three end products of this treatment?
   (c) What are the uses of each of these end products?

6 What are the advantages of using the deep shaft process of waste water treatment compared with the activated sludge process?

7 In the 1950s detergent foams often floated on rivers. This is not the case nowadays. Why?

8 Why has the salmon returned to the River Thames?

CHAPTER 6
BIOTECHNOLOGY, HEALTH AND DISEASE

Much recent work in biotechnology has been in the health industry, which is big business. In simple terms *health* means *without disease*.

The causes of some diseases such as cancer are not well understood. Other diseases such as *diabetes* occur due to an imbalance in the body's natural chemistry. In this section, however, we will concentrate on the prevention and cure of those human and animal diseases caused by microbes. When some microbes invade the body they cause disease.

The *germ theory* of disease was confirmed in the late nineteenth century by two famous scientists – Robert Koch in Germany and Louis Pasteur in France. They proved that certain diseases are caused by certain microbes. One type of microbe will cause smallpox, for example, but another type will cause cholera.

Robert Koch

Louis Pasteur

Before the 1870s many strange and 'supernatural' attempts were made to explain diseases. Since that time a more scientific approach to the treatment of diseases has developed. It is now known that many common diseases are caused by bacteria, fungi or viruses.

These diseases may spread, being passed from person to person. Once infectious microbes have been identified attempts are made to 'fight them off'. Luckily only about 13% of known microbes, given the right conditions, are potentially harmful. Biotechnologists can use some of the remaining 87% to produce medicines which will help to prevent and cure diseases and so keep people and animals healthy.

It is important to realise at this stage that biotechnology – in the area of health – is restricted to the *production* of useful *medicines*. These include antibiotics and vaccines. Neither the *use* of medicines in treatment nor *medical engineering*, e.g. development of artificial hip joints and heart pace-makers, is included in biotechnology.

ANTIBIOTICS

Many of the developments made in modern biotechnology are based on experience gained from the production of antibiotics. This has occurred on a large scale since the 1940s. Antibiotics are chemicals used to prevent or cure a disease. They may be given as *injections*, in solid form as *tablets* or in liquid form as *medicines*. They destroy the harmful microbes causing the disease *without* harming the patient. Nowadays there are about 100 different antibiotics available for use by humans. The most well-known of these is *penicillin*.

The discovery of penicillin

Penicillin was the first antibiotic to be discovered. In 1928 Alexander Fleming was studying the growth of bacteria on jelly in glass dishes at his laboratory in a London hospital. One day he noticed that a mould, *Penicillium notatum*, was growing in one of the dishes. He guessed that the mould must have settled from the air and contaminated the dish. The growth of bacteria was poor near the mould, but further away from it colonies of bacteria were larger. Fleming correctly suggested that the mould was preventing the growth of bacteria. The chemical causing this effect was extracted and called *penicillin*.

Alexander Fleming

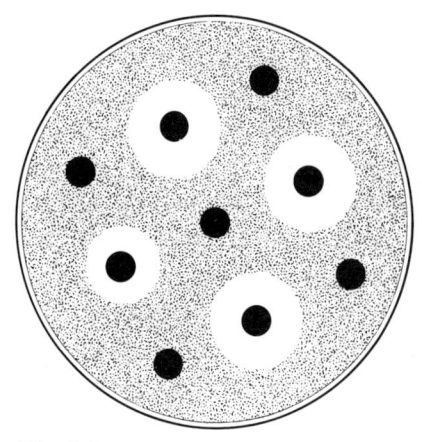

'Clear' rings appear around microbes which produce antibiotics

It is now known that some naturally occurring chemicals can control the growth of many disease-forming microbes. These substances are called *antibiotics* (*anti* means 'against'; *biotic* means 'living things'). Antibiotics work against some other living things and destroy them. The fungi, a group to which moulds belong, and some bacteria are important producers of antibiotics.

Fleming had made an important scientific discovery about a property possessed by a living organism. This is the first and most crucial step in *most* developments in biotechnology.

It was not Fleming, however, but a group of scientists at Oxford University who, ten years later, picked up this idea and attempted to put it into practical use. By 1943 penicillin was being produced on a relatively large scale. It saved many lives during World War II. Many wounded soldiers who were suffering from infections caused by bacteria were treated with penicillin.

The production of penicillin

During the early days of penicillin the moulds were grown as colonies on the surface of jelly inside glass flasks or even in milk bottles. Only small yields of the antibiotic were obtained. Perhaps 50 mg of penicillin could be extracted from a one litre flask full of the mould and its food. The process was also very labour-intensive as large numbers of people were needed to clean or sterilise the containers ready for re-use.

In nature, not all members of the same species or type of organism are alike. They show *variations*, even in a similar characteristic. Consider members of your class at school. Some are tall, others are short. There is probably a whole range of heights within the group, even though they all belong to the same species and are a similar age.

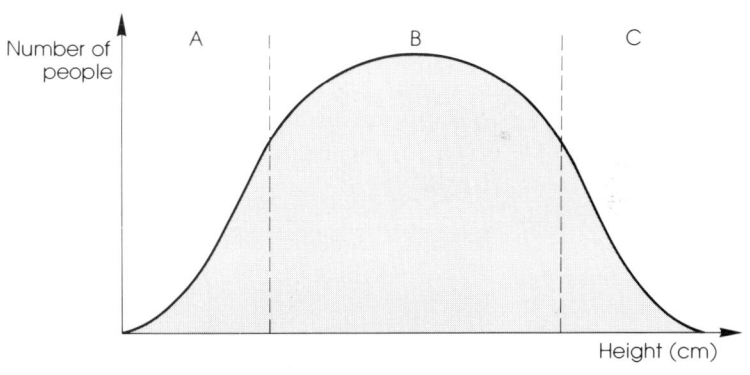

Try carrying out a survey of heights in your class; see whether your graph looks like this

Most people are of average height (B), fewer are short (A) or tall (C)

Similarly variations occur in microbes. Early workers in penicillin production looked at many *Penicillium* moulds. They tried to find out which types (species) produced relatively large amounts of penicillin. These were chosen for further development, to try for still larger amounts.

Once a type of mould was found which produced large amounts of penicillin, experiments with X-rays and ultra-violet light were used to make further improvements. Those organisms which gave even *higher* yields of penicillin were then selected and the others discarded.

Penicillin production from one type of *Penicillium*, following experiments with X-rays and UV light

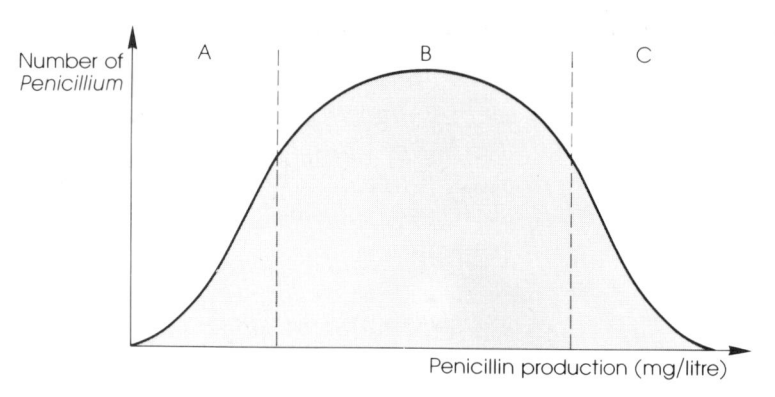

Most moulds produce average quantities of penicillin (B)
A few moulds produce small quantities of penicillin (A)
Others produce large quantities of penicillin (C)
Of the three groups, A, B and C, which group would the biotechnologist choose for further penicillin production?

Which two groups would be discarded?

As a result of such work similar quantities of moulds nowadays can produce *10 000 times as much antibiotic*, compared with those in the early days of penicillin production.

Also, the original mould would grow only on the surface of the jelly containing food. Types of mould were later chosen which would grow successfully submerged in a liquid *broth*. This meant that large-scale production could be carried out efficiently in massive fermenters, rather than using small glass containers.

Modern antibiotic production, including penicillin, is carried out by using high-yielding moulds submerged in liquid *culture* (broth) inside large steel fermenters.

(a) Penicillin production in the 1940s

(b) Penicillin production in the 1980s

(a)

(b)

Use of antibiotics

Initially penicillin was thought to be *the* wonder drug which would cure all diseases. It *can* cure a wide range of diseases caused by bacteria, but there are three major problems. One is that some diseases such as tuberculosis (TB) do not respond to penicillin. Secondly, some people are *allergic* to penicillin. Thirdly, bacteria became resistant to penicillin after continual use.

After a few years of using penicillin doctors found that some infections which had previously been cured did not respond to treatment. These new *resistant* strains of disease-causing microbes were difficult to kill. One solution to this problem is to allow the body's *natural defences* to fight against common illnesses. As a result less penicillin is used and fewer resistant strains of microbes develop. Another solution, especially if resistant strains of microbes *have* developed, is to discover new types of antibiotics.

So far about 5000 chemicals have been isolated from microbes which have been shown to kill other microbes. From these about 100 different antibiotics are available. The rest have been rejected because they have harmful side-effects or are too expensive to manufacture on a large scale. Collectively these antibiotics form a multi-million pound business worldwide.

Penicillin, cephalosporin and streptomycin are three common antibiotics in general use:

- **Penicillin**   Kills a number of disease-causing bacteria.
- **Cephalosporin**   Tackles diseases such as *pneumonia* caused by penicillin-resistant microbes.
- **Streptomycin**   Attacks microbes unharmed by penicillin and cephalosporin. It has been useful in the treatment of tuberculosis.

It can be seen from this simple example that a doctor has a range of antibiotics available to treat different kinds of disease.

CASE STUDY 16

Antibiotic production

1 Finding the microbe

Scientists are constantly looking for new strains of microbes which may make useful products such as antibiotics. *Penicillium*, the mould which makes penicillin, was discovered by chance, in a laboratory. Many antibiotic producers are found growing in soil. The organism *Cephalosporium* was isolated off the coast of Sardinia in 1945. It took 17 years and the development of many new strains of this microbe, though, before an antibiotic was ready for use in humans. This antibiotic was *cephalosporin*.

Once isolated, a productive strain of microbe is preserved by freeze-drying. It can then be stored for years if necessary.

2 Fermentation and growth

Test-tubes

To start production by fermentation, the microbe – which has been preserved as a pellet in a small tube – is reactivated with sterile water. It is then *streaked* on to the surface of agar jelly in test-tubes. The jelly provides the nutrients on which the microbe feeds.

Wastes

The microbe will grow and reproduce only if it has warmth and food. Then it converts the *nutrients* (food) into waste products. An antibiotic is one of these waste products – with life-saving properties.

As found in nature, microbes produce only small amounts of antibiotics. Only after much research and selection can some organisms be encouraged to increase their *yield*.

Flasks

After growing inside test-tubes for a few days, the antibiotic producers are transferred, under sterile conditions, into *flasks*, where they grow in a liquid nutrient. The flasks are shaken continuously to encourage the microbes to spread throughout the liquid.

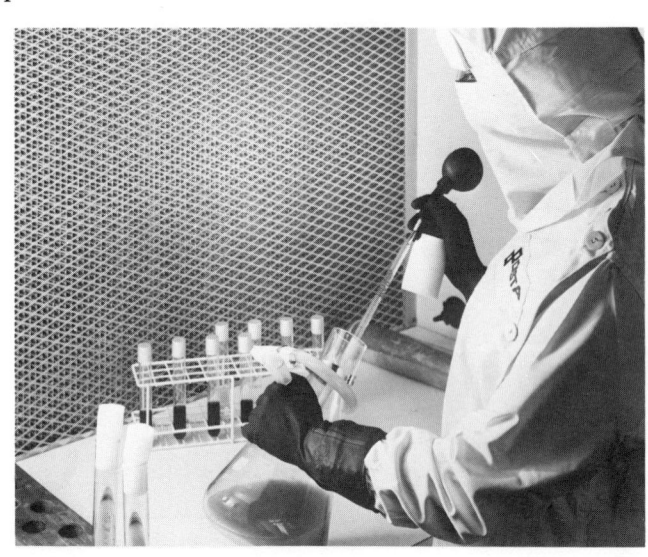

Micro-organisms are transferred under sterile conditions

The storage of liquid at the raw materials Dista Products plant, Liverpool

The tops of giant fermenter vessels at the Dista Products plant, Liverpool

Filtration of mycelium and unused solid nutrients

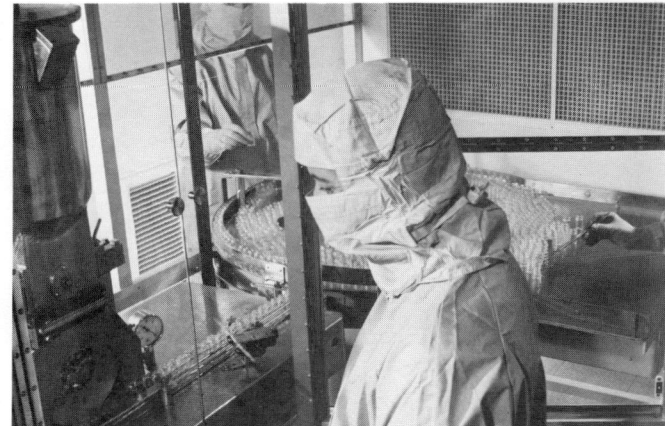

Small containers are filled under sterile conditions

Inspection of equipment used in the manufacture of antibiotics

The end products

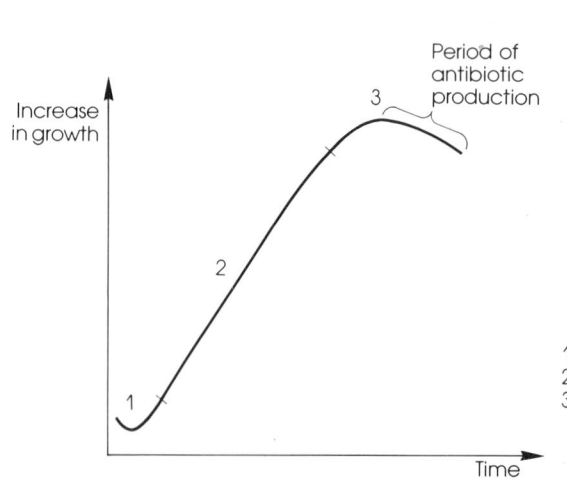

A typical growth curve

1 Initial growth – little, if any, growth occurs
2 Period of rapid growth
3 Decline in rate of growth followed by death of the organism.
Antibiotics are produced only in stage 3 of the life cycle of the microbes which produce them.

Fermenters

Rapid growth starts at this stage and a thread-like mass develops. This means that the nutrient is used up. The microbes are then transferred through a series of increasingly larger fermenters. These are stainless steel tanks in which the growth of the microbes continues on an ever-increasing scale.

(i) **Seed vessel**   The first, which is called the *seed vessel*, is full of liquid food which has been sterilised to destroy unwanted organisms. It has a stirrer to keep the contents moving, a supply of sterile air to provide oxygen for respiration, steam for additional warmth and chilled water-coils to remove excess heat.

(ii) **Larger vessel**   When the desired growth is reached in the seed vessel, the contents are transferred to a larger vessel containing more nutrients, to allow more growth.

(iii) **Final tank**   Final tanks have volumes up to 250 000 litres. These vessels are fitted with powerful stirrers and are aerated throughout the fermentation. The temperature and pH inside these tanks are carefully controlled. Also, to maintain the best growing conditions, solid nutrients may be added.

Why different stages?

We have already talked about scaling up from smaller to larger growth vessels in a series of gradual steps. In the production of antibiotics, the required product – the antibiotic – is only produced during a certain stage of the microbe's life cycle. It is essential that millions of organisms should be growing in the antibiotic-growing phase *at the same time*, so that there is enough concentration for *harvest* and *recovery*.

Product recovery

Eventually the nutrients are all used up and the rate of production of antibiotic slows down. It is then time to *harvest* the antibiotic. The contents of the fermenter vessel are transferred to a recovery area. Here the solid materials, consisting of unused solid nutrients and the mycelium are removed by filtration. The antibiotic is left behind.

In order to recover the antibiotic, it may be dissolved in a suitable liquid and then dried, to form crystals.

Processing

The partially pure antibiotic is now processed further until it is pure enough to be used in the human body. The pure product is made into *tablets* or *capsules*.

Biosynthesis

Sometimes the compound recovered from the fermenter is too weak. In other cases it may not have the right properties to be an effective antibiotic in itself. In either case the naturally fermented substance may be developed, using chemistry, to produce a new and useful compound. This process is called *biosynthesis*.

VACCINES

It is always better to prevent disease rather than cure it. One way to help prevent some *non-infectious diseases* is to keep fit and active. Vaccines can be used to prevent some *infectious diseases* which are caused by microbes.

The first work on vaccination was carried out in the late 18th century by Edward Jenner, in England. At that time *smallpox* was a common disease. *Cowpox* was a similar, but less severe, disease sometimes caught by milkmaids who handled cows. Jenner noticed that people who had suffered from cowpox did not catch smallpox.

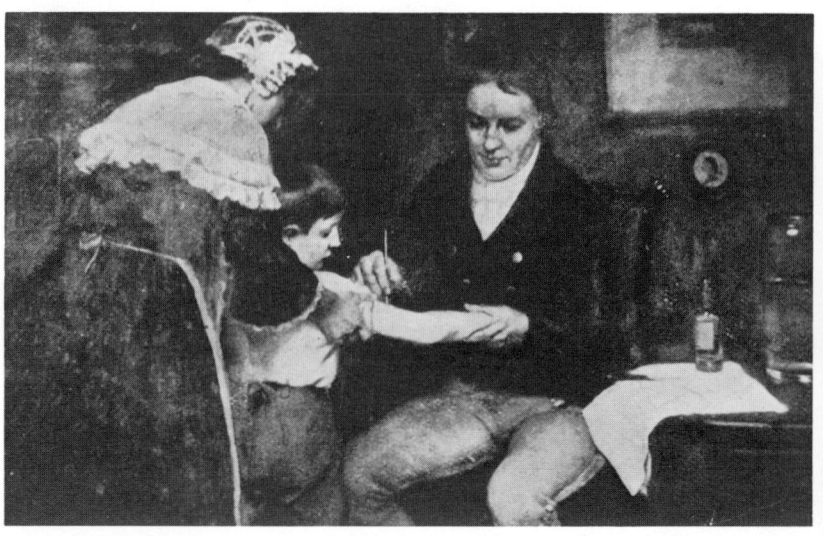

Edward Jenner performed the first vaccination

In a daring experiment – which would *never* be tried nowadays – Jenner took some of the pus from spots on a milkmaid suffering from cowpox and inoculated the arm of a healthy boy with it. The boy caught cowpox. When the boy recovered, Jenner inoculated him with smallpox. The boy did not however catch smallpox. He had been made immune to the disease. Similar tests with a number of people showed that exposure to cowpox resulted in immunity from smallpox.

Jenner was therefore the first person to show that vaccination could protect against a disease. Later work by Louis Pasteur established how vaccines prevent disease.

How vaccines prevent disease

The body has its own natural defences against disease. Vaccines work by stimulating this defence system. When microbial cells enter the body certain white blood cells produce proteins called *antibodies*.

The microbial cells have, as part of their disease-causing system, other proteins called *antigens*. Antibodies in the body fight against the invading antigens and join with them. This acts as a signal to other white blood cells to engulf the antibody-antigen complexes. Once the effect of the harmful microbes is removed the disease is prevented.

In simple terms if there are more antibodies than antigens then the body remains healthy.

Certain antibodies will only join with certain antigens. An antibody will only join with an antigen which has exactly the right shape. They are *specific*. This means that one type of antibody will prevent one kind of disease. Vaccines work by stimulating the production of antibodies in the body, so that if microbial antigens invade they will be destroyed before any harm can be done.

The vaccines themselves may be made from weakened living microbes which cause the disease. This is similar to the cowpox/smallpox situation. Other types of vaccines contain dead microbes or poisons from microbes that would have caused the disease. Vaccines may be taken *orally* (through the mouth), as with 'sugar-lump' vaccinations against polio, or by *injections*. Once the body has been stimulated by a vaccine some of the antibodies produced will remain in the bloodstream and bring about long-term protection against that disease. If the same type of microbe later attempts to invade the body it is immediately destroyed by the presence of the antibodies.

Production of hepatitis B vaccine

Protection from disease is called *immunity*. Natural immunity occurs when a person has had a mild attack of a disease. This stimulates the body's defence system to give protection against further attacks. Vaccination results in *artificial immunity*. Very young children are commonly vaccinated against diphtheria, tetanus and whooping cough. Older children are vaccinated against polio, measles and tuberculosis. In most cases *booster* injections are necessary to stimulate antibody production and increase protection.

Although German measles is a mild disease, girls in their teens are vaccinated against it. This is because if a pregnant woman is exposed to the disease, permanent damage to the child may result.

In recent years some parents have chosen not to have their children vaccinated against whooping cough. This is because this particular vaccine may cause permanent brain damage in a very small percentage of people who are given it.

Vaccines have played an important part in the prevention of many harmful diseases. Some of these, such as smallpox, have been completely eradicated. Much of the recent work in vaccine development has been against diseases caused by viruses. Soon we may be offered protection against common viral diseases such as colds and 'flu.

CASE STUDY 17

Magic bullets

The ideal drugs would be like *magic bullets*. They would have no side effects and would move to the *exact* place in the body where they were needed. *Monoclonal antibodies* (MABs) are sometimes called magic bullets. They were discovered in 1975 by scientists working at Cambridge University. Of all the new biotechnologies it is thought that those which use MABs will have the biggest impact on medicine. But what are *antibodies* and what does *monoclonal* mean?

Antibodies
Antibodies help protect against infection. They are made by cells in the body in response to attack by microbes.

If antibody-producing cells are grown in the laboratory, instead of the body, large amounts of antibody can be made. These are known as MABs.

What does monoclonal mean?
A *clone* is a large number of identical cells. *Monoclonal* means a clone produced from one type of cell.

Where are antibodies made?
Antibodies are made by special kinds of *white blood cells*. Most are made in the *lymph* nodes of the body, e.g. under the armpit. The cells which make antibodies are called *lymphocytes*.

How do antibodies work?
There are proteins on the surface of every microbe. These proteins have a unique shape and are called *antigens*. Antibodies have shapes which allow them to join with antigens. When they join, antibodies make antigens harmless.

Making antibodies
The body is usually invaded by many microbes of the same type at any one time. In order to prevent infection many lymphocytes must be made in the body quickly. These produce antibodies which join with antigens to prevent infection.

MABs
Lymphocytes reproduce quickly inside the body in response to microbial invasion. During MAB production scientists grow a certain type of lymphocyte *outside* the body. This one type of lymphocyte makes one type of antibody – a MAB.

Making MABs in the laboratory
Lymphocytes quickly die outside the body. They can, however, go on living and dividing in the laboratory if they are joined to certain cancer cells. Cancer cells are able to grow and divide quickly inside the body and under certain laboratory conditions. Lymphocytes joined with cancer cells are called *hybrid* cells. These hybrid cells can live outside the body like cancer cells *and* make antibodies like lymphocytes. From these hybrids MABs can be made.

Monoclonal antibody production
Step 1 Spleen cell and cancer cell are joined
Step 2 Hybridoma cells are cloned
Step 3 Hybridoma cells are cultured
Step 4 MABs are extracted from the culture vessel

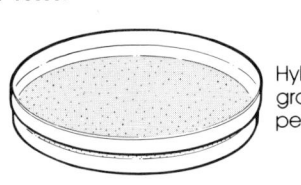

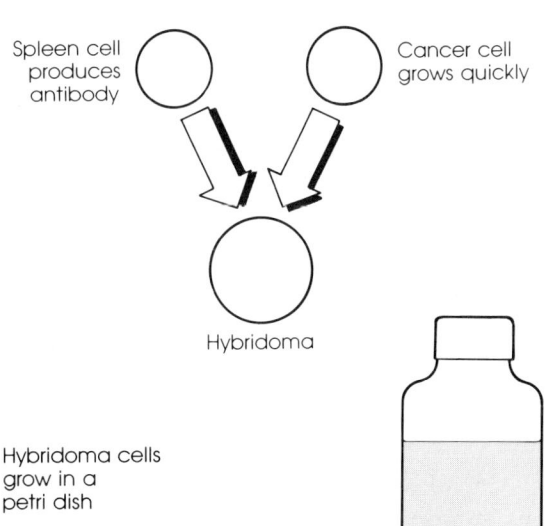

Spleen cell produces antibody

Cancer cell grows quickly

Hybridoma

Hybridoma cells grow in a petri dish

Hybridoma cells grow quickly in a culture vessel. They produce MABs

Magic bullets – hitting the target

Antibodies work by recognising a protein on the surface of a certain kind of cell and joining with it. It could be said that the antibody attacks a *target*. A MAB will attack one kind of target cell only.

If a drug is attached to a MAB then the antibody can hit its target – a diseased cell. The drug would be taken to the diseased cell by the antibody. In this way the drug can act exactly where it is needed in the body.

Chemical detectives

As well as helping to cure disease MABs can also be used as chemical detectives to detect disease quickly and accurately. Nowadays kits can be made which allow diseases to be detected easily. These kits contain MABs which join with antigens on the surface of the disease-causing microbe.

A solution containing MABs is added to a sample of the patient's urine or blood. If microbes are present the antibodies react with them. This causes a chemical in the test to change colour, which shows that the patient has the disease.

Big business

The possible uses of MABs in treatment and detection of disease are great. Some estimates suggest that, by the late 1980s, the worldwide market for MABs will be about £500 million.

Biotechnology *is* big business. It also offers exciting possibilities in the future!

SUMMARY

Some chemicals can help keep us healthy. *Antibiotics* kill off harmful disease-causing microbes without harming body cells. They are used to prevent or cure a disease. *Vaccines* build up artificial immunity to diseases. They do this by stimulating the body's defence system to fight off invading microbes which are potentially harmful. They are used to prevent diseases occurring.

Monoclonal antibodies have been discovered recently. They act like *magic bullets* and travel to precise sites in the body where they can be used to detect or cure diseases.

The health area of biotechnology is big business. It is involved with the production of useful medicines including antibiotics, vaccines and MABs.

ACTIVITY 15

Penicillin production

The mould *Penicillium* was grown in a large fermenter. As a result penicillin was made. Changes inside the fermenter were monitored over a five-day period. The weight of the mould per litre and amount of antibiotic were recorded.

Time (hours)	Density of Penicillium (g/l)	Amount of penicillin (units/ml)
0	4	0
20	20	0
40	36	5
60	42	20
80	38	32
100	32	48
120	30	46

Graph the results e.g.

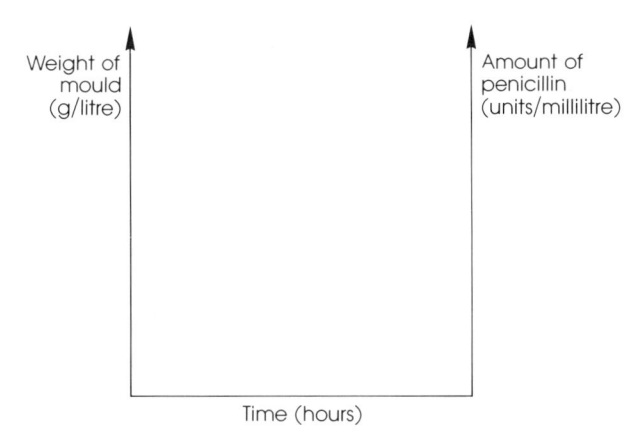

Weight of mould (g/litre) vs Time (hours)

Amount of penicillin (units/millilitre) vs Time (hours)

The increase in weight over a five-day period corresponds to a typical growth curve. Explain.

From your knowledge of the life cycle of *Penicillium* try to explain why:

1) very little antibiotic is produced during the first 40 hours,

2) there is a rapid production of antibiotic between 40 and 100 hours.

From the graph, predict when is the best time to harvest the mould in order to extract the penicillin.

ACTIVITY 16

Helping Y-US

Y-US is a small remote village in a Third World country. The people are starving. Their water supplies are polluted. Their fuel supplies are limited. They suffer from disease.

It is possible that biotechnology can be used to help them.

1) How, by using 'low-tech' cheap, primitive biotechnological processes can they attempt to 'help themselves'?

2) Which aspects of modern industrial biotechnology can be used to help them?

Try to explain your answers to 1) and 2) as fully as possible. Mention advantages and disadvantages of both approaches.

During the next 20 years or so, will biotechnology be used to help Third World populations or rich western populations? Why?

ACTIVITY 17 — Using a key to distinguish between products of biotechnology

Here is an example.

Common microbial food can be distinguished by asking three basic questions.

- Is an acid made?
- Is alcohol made?
- What type of fermentation process is involved?

1) In production is an acid made?
   Yes   see 2
   No   see 4

2) Is it acetic acid?
   Yes   vinegar   pickles
   No   see 3

3) Is it lactic acid?
   Yes   products include: **butter, cheese, sauerkraut, yoghurt, silage (animal food).**
   No   glutamic acid: lysine = food additives

4) In production is alcohol made?
   Yes   from apples   **cider**
         from malted barley   **beer**
         from grape juice   **wine**
   No   see 5

5) Is a complex fermentation process involved?
   Yes   **soy sauce**
   No   see 6

6) Microbes used directly as food   **yeast extract, single cell protein e.g. Pruteen**

   Gas produced   **bread**

Apart from microbial foods other 'products' of biotechnology include:
plastics, antibiotics, biogas, vaccines, fuel alcohol, metals, water, enzymes, MABs, plants (from tissue culture), composts, insulin.

Can you devise your own key in order to organise these products in an appropriate manner?

Is your key similar to that of other pupils in your group?
Is it possible that a 'correct answer' can be obtained by using different approaches?
How important are the basic questions that you ask when devising the key?

QUESTIONS ON CHAPTER 6

1. In simple terms what does 'health' mean?
2. (a) What is the 'germ theory of disease'?
   (b) What two scientists confirmed this theory?
   (c) How are diseases spread?
   (d) What percentage of microbes may potentially cause disease?
   (e) Give one way in which biotechnologists can use the remaining 'harmless' microbes.
3. What area of health is biotechnology restricted to?
4. (a) What are antibiotics?
   (b) How do they work?
5. Briefly outline how penicillin was:
   (a) discovered,
   (b) first produced on an industrial scale.
6. (a) How do biotechnologists increase yields of products?
   (b) How does the yield of a modern-day *Penicillium* mould compare with those types used during the 1940s?
7. (a) What is meant by
      (i) surface culture? (ii) submerged liquid culture?
   (b) Which of these two types are used in modern antibiotic production? Why?
8. (a) Name three groups of antibiotics in common use.
   (b) Give an example how they may be used to treat different kinds of diseases.

9 'An important scientific discovery about a property possessed by a living organism is the first step in most developments in biotechnology.'
  (a) What was the first step in:
    (i) penicillin production?   (ii) vaccine production?
  (b) In each case, which scientist made the discovery?

10 How do vaccines prevent disease?

11 Name five diseases which you can be vaccinated against.

12 Why do you need 'booster' injections from time to time?

13 What are 'monoclonal antibodies'? How do they work?

14 Write briefly about the part played by antibiotics, vaccinations and MABs in the 'prevention and cure of disease'.

WORDMAZE ON BIOTECHNOLOGY, HEALTH AND DISEASE

The wordmaze contains all the words listed below but not in this order. Can you find your way around? You can only use each letter once and you cannot go diagonally. The last letter of each word is followed by the first letter of the next word. The first word is VIRUS.

```
             U O I N I I M N A T A C I N
             S S T F G N E U T E N Y T U
             R T C E R F L S R E C I M M
             E P T N E N I A N E S G U Ⓥ—Start
             I C O N S E C I T I P D R I
    Finish—Ⓝ Y M E J D I B O D A S U R
             U M O A T E M S R T S E N I
             E N N I B E S M U E R P I C
             A P O H D T E A P O E T L L
             R E L C I A B L L X A N N I
             I O O X V Y T G I T N E A N
             L C P C A N I E N E R M I T
             O O W C M U A R S F S C B I
             P E N I M I L U T A N I T O
```

antibodies	medicines
antibiotics	natural immunity
antigens	Pasteur
cancer	penicillin
cholera	pneumonia
cowpox	polio
diabetes	streptomycin
drug	smallpox
Fleming	TB
fermenter	tetanus
infectious	vaccine
immunity	virus
Jenner	

FURTHER READING

TEXTBOOKS

Bishop, O. *Adventures with microorganisms* (John Murray, 1984)
Teasdale, J. *Microbes* (Macdonald, 1984)

Interesting, but more advanced reading

Dixon, B. *Invisible allies* (Temple Smith, 1976)
Yoxen, E. *The Gene Business* (Pan, 1983)

BOOKLETS PRODUCED BY INDUSTRIAL ORGANISATIONS

Company/organisation	*Name of booklet/information sheet*
ICI Agricultural division PO Box 1 Billingham Cleveland	*Pruteen* A colourful, well-illustrated booklet which gives information on the company, biotechnology, the product, testing trials, and the fermentation process in the production of this high protein food made by growing bacteria on methanol. *Steam* A new science teachers' magazine. Circulated free to all secondary schools. Additional copies from: ICI Educational Publications, P.O. Box 96, 1, Hornchurch Close, Coventry, West Midlands CV1 2QZ.
Harwell AERE Harwell Oxfordshire OX11 0RA	*The promise of biotechnology.* Contains some clear, precise information sheets on topics including immobilised enzyme technology.

Gist Brocades PO Box 1 2600MA Delft Holland	*Biotechnology Today* A well-illustrated colourful document which includes articles on the history of biotechnology, DNA research, the importance of scale up, the food industry, biological detergents and enzymes. *Taking a Look at the Invisible* The illustrations are excellent, the text relates mostly to company products.
National Dairy Council John Princes Street London WIM 6AP	*Facts about Soft Cheese, Facts about Yoghurt* and *Champion Cheese* Three information booklets, e.g. *Champion Cheese* gives a well-illustrated account of the stages in the industrial production of cheese. *Dairy Education* A regular informative (free) newspaper which is circulated to schools.
Novo Ringway House Bell Road Daneshill East Basingstoke Hampshire	*Enzymes at Work* A thorough and detailed look at all aspects of enzymes in relation to industrial applications. General accounts are given of industrial processes which are then related to specific company products. Articles include: baking industry, dairy industry, detergent industry, leather industry, wine and fruit juice industry, starch industry, textile industry, protein industry and pharmaceutical industry.
RHM Lincoln Road, High Wycombe Bucks. HP12 3QR	*Mycoprotein – a new food* A paper which investigates the feasibility of large scale production of a new human food from a fungus.

Tate and Lyle
Philip Lyle
Memorial Research Lab.
White Knights
Reading
Berkshire

Biotechnology in the 80s A well-illustrated booklet which has articles on enzyme technology, ethanol production, effluent treatment, crop protection and fish and algal culture.

Recent information sheets on:
- transformed sucrose
- microbial pesticides
- talin protein production
- isomaltulose
- sugar processing
- solidified glucose

Unilever
Unilever House
Blackfriars
London
EC4 4BQ

Clonal Oil-Palm: propagation by tissue culture A well-illustrated colourful booklet on the research and development of oil palms using cloning techniques.

Unilever Sheet. Topics No 9. The SCSST lecture. *Biotechnology – What is it – Where is it going?* By Sir G. Allen, Director of Research and Engineering. Unilever also produce a wide range of other books related to industry.

ANSWERS

Answers to crossword on living things and industrial processes

Across

2 pH
4 Scum
7 DNA
8 Exit
10 Scaling up
12 Growth
15 Hot
16 Neutral
17 Gas
19 Bar
20 Parasite
22 Batch
23 Isomerase
28 Agar
29 Life
31 Enzyme
32 Proteases
33 Start

Down

1 Oxygen
3 Host
5 Cells
6 Mineral
7 Dough
9 Two
11 Cheats
13 Water
14 Starch
18 Engineers
19 Bath
20 Protozoa
21 Air
24 Sugar
25 Broth
26 Algae
27 Emit
30 Fuel

Answers to wordfinder on biotechnology and fuels

1 Wood
2 Alcohol
3 Heat
4 Fuel
5 Yeast
6 Distillation
7 Gasohol
8 Cassava
9 Coal
10 Reservoir
11 Biomass
12 Xanthan gum
13 Production
14 Sugar
15 Methane
16 Oil
17 Brazil
18 Gas
19 Energy
20 Enzyme

Answers to wordmaze on biotechnology, health and disease

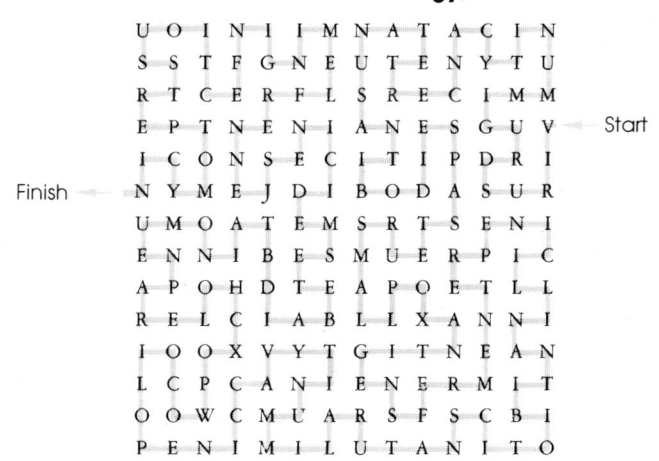

```
              U O I N I I M N A T A C I N
              S S T F G N E U T E N Y T U
              R T C E R F L S R E C I M M
              E P T N E N I A N E S G U V  — Start
              I C O N S E C I T I P D R I
Finish —      N Y M E J D I B O D A S U R
              U M O A T E M S R T S E N I
              E N N I B E S M U E R P I C
              A P O H D T E A P O E T L L
              R E L C I A B L L X A N N I
              I O O X V Y T G I T N E A N
              L C P C A N I E N E R M I T
              O O W C M U A R S F S C B I
              P E N I M I L U T A N I T O
```

117

INDEX

Acid   26, 28, 43
Agar   7, 100
Alcohol   11, 29, 33, 47, 67, 70, 71, 77, 78
Algae   31, 32, 42, 49, 88
Alkaline   26, 28
Animals   1, 9, 12, 32, 42, 64, 73
Antibiotic   13, 17, 23, 96–103, 108–10
Antibodies   105–8
Antigens   105
Artificial immunity   106

Bacteria   11, 16, 17, 21, 31, 43, 44, 45, 48, 50, 51, 61, 72–4, 79, 80, 81, 94, 96
Barley   46
Batch fermenter   36, 37
Beer   10, 11, 23, 27, 29, 36, 42, 45–7, 48, 52–4
Biogas   71–3, 75, 81
Biology   1, 4, 25
Biomas   65–7
Biotechnology   1, 2, 4–6, 10, 11, 19–21, 23, 25, 30, 31, 33, 37, 42, 52, 65, 67, 70, 81, 85, 91, 94–6, 108, 110
Bread   10, 11, 23, 27, 28, 42, 44, 45, 47
Broth   13, 36, 98

Cancer   107
Carbohydrate   65
Carbon dioxide   11, 31–3, 44, 71, 72
Cassava   71
Catalyst   25, 26
Cell   1, 2, 6, 7, 12, 14, 16–8, 21, 25, 26, 29, 31, 34, 37, 38, 51, 105, 106, 108
Cephalosporin   99
Chemicals   2, 19
Cheese   11, 42–4, 47, 48, 55, 58, 59
Chlorophyll   32
Chromosome   14, 16
Clone   17, 106
Coal   64, 65
Computer   20, 21, 38
Continuous fermenter   36, 37
Crops   68, 71
Culture   6, 98
Curds   43, 49

Decay   32
Diabetes   15, 94
Diet   15
Disease   21, 95, 105, 106
DNA   9, 13, 16, 21, 25
Downstream processing   17
Drug   10, 13, 106

Energy   31–3, 64, 65, 67, 71
Engineer   21, 37
Enzyme   12, 16, 25, 26–31, 33, 38, 46–8, 55
Ethanol   66–71, 77
Extinct   8

Famine   21
Fermentation   11, 67, 71, 74, 100
Fermenter   5, 13, 33–8, 52, 61, 72, 73, 90, 98, 103
Flask   100
Fleming   13, 96, 97
Flour   44, 45
Food   2, 6, 7, 10, 11, 18, 25, 31–4, 36, 37, 42, 47, 49, 50, 52, 60, 98, 100
Fuel   2, 6, 10, 19, 25, 64–6, 68–73, 77–81, 87, 89
Fungi   32, 50, 88, 94, 96

Gasohol   69
Genes   9, 14, 16–8, 21
Genetic engineering   9, 10, 14, 17–21, 48

Health   42, 77, 94–112
Heredity   14, 18
Hormone   15
Host   16, 17, 32

Immobilisation   29
Immunity   104, 108
Industrialist   33
Insulin   14–6, 18, 21

Jenner   104

Koch   94

Landfill   75

118

Malt   46–7
Medicines   2, 95, 108
Methane   66, 71–4, 87
Microbes   1, 2, 4, 9, 11, 12, 14, 17–9, 36, 42, 47, 49, 51, 52, 72, 81, 85, 88, 94, 99, 100, 105, 106
Microbiology   4
Microscope   2, 11, 14
Milk   11–3, 43, 49, 52–8, 97
Minerals   32, 49, 50
Monoclonal antibodies   106–8
Mould   11, 13, 32, 97, 98, 109

Natural immunity   106
Neutral   26, 28
Nucleic acid   51
Nucleus   9, 14
Nutrients   37, 80

Oil   6, 7, 19, 64, 65, 68, 73, 77–80
Oxygen   11, 31–7, 67, 80

Pancreas   15, 18
Parasite   32
Pasteur   12, 94, 104
Pasteurised   43, 55
Penicillin   13, 36, 95–9, 109, 110
Penicillium   13, 97, 110
pH   28, 29, 34, 36, 37, 50, 54, 57
Photosynthesis   31, 32, 65, 80
Pilot plant   33, 34, 37
Plants   1, 6–8, 12, 21, 23, 31, 32, 42, 64, 65, 78, 80, 81
Plasmids   16, 17
Pollution   2, 21, 85, 91
Protein   25, 43, 49, 50, 52, 55, 60
Protozoa   31, 32, 88

Raw materials   38
Reactor vessel   30
Rennet   43, 57
Respiration   32, 67

Saprophyte   32
Scaling up   33
Sewage   32, 85, 86–90
Smallpox   104
Spontaneous generation   11
Starter   43, 44, 48
Sterilise   38, 61
Streptomycin   99
Substrate   26, 31
Sugar   27, 29, 30, 45–7, 67–9, 71, 78

Technology   1, 48
Tissue culture   6–8

Vaccine   104–6
Vinegar   11, 45
Virus   94
Vitamins   49

Warmth   26, 27, 31, 34, 36, 37, 52
Water   2, 17, 22, 31, 46, 55, 73, 79, 80, 85–93, 109
Whey   43, 49
Wine   11, 12
Wort   47

Xanthan gum   79

Yeast   11, 29, 33, 44, 67, 70, 71
Yoghurt   11, 47, 48, 54, 55

Text © J Teasdale 1987
Illustrations © Stanley Thornes (Publishers) Ltd 1987

All rights reserved. No part* of this publication by be reproduced, stored in a retrieval system or transmitted in any form or by any means, electronic, mechanical, photocopying, recording or otherwise, without the prior written consent of the copyright holders. Applications for such permission should be addressed to the publishers: Stanley Thornes (Publishers) Ltd, Old Station Drive, Leckhampton, CHELTENHAM GL53 0DN, England.

First published in 1987 by
Stanley Thornes (Publishers) Ltd
Old Station Drive
Leckhampton
CHELTENHAM GL53 0DN
England

Reprinted 1988

*An exception is made for the word puzzles on pp. 40, 84 and 113. Teachers may photocopy a puzzle to save time for a pupil who would otherwise need to copy from his/her copy of the book. Teachers wishing to make multiple copies of a word puzzle for distribution to a class without individual copies of the book must apply to the publishers in the normal way.

British Library Cataloguing in Publication Data
Teasdale, Jim
   Biotechnology.—(Extending science).
   1.   Biotechnology
   I. Title   II. Series
   660'.6   TP248.2

ISBN 0-85950-555-3

Typeset by Tech-Set, Gateshead, Tyne & Wear.
Printed and bound in Great Britain at The Bath Press, Avon.